BRAIN GAMES®

MOST WANTED

CRIME PUZZLES

pi

Publications International, Ltd.

Introduction

Fugitives fascinate us—those stories of people who fled before they could face justice. If you're a crime aficionado, this collection delivers more than 125 puzzles themed around crime, the FBI's Most Wanted List, and famous, infamous, and obscure fugitives. Exercise your brain and solve an assortment of puzzles.

- See if DNA sequences are a match

- View crime scenes and answer questions about them

- Untangle cryptograms about fugitives

- Challenge your spatial skills as you solve mazes

- Test your observational skills with word searches

- Have fun with wordplay as you solve word ladders and anagrams

- Use your logic skills to track down the cities where the fugitive visited, pin down which motel room they're hiding in, and more

Some puzzles you'll solve right away. For others, you might need to set them aside for a while before returning to them. And if you get really stuck, there's always an answer key at the back.

So grab a pencil, get ready to track down answers, and get started.

Change just one letter on each line to go from the top word to the bottom word. Do not change the order of the letters. You must have a common English word at each step.

MOST

_____

_____

_____

WANT

GOES

_____

_____

_____

_____

FREE

4

Answers on page 178.

You've intercepted a message between a criminal who fled and his accomplice. But the message doesn't seem to make sense! Can you discover the criminal's current location hidden in the message?

CAN HE ARRANGE RED LIGHT OR TWO TIMES ELECTRICITY, NEXT CENTURY?

Escape the Building

Can you escape this circular building or will you be caught?

Answer on page 178.

Crime Anagrams

Unscramble each word or phrase below to reveal a word or phrase related to the Most Wanted list.

I GUT FIVE

ERUPT CAD

ACE MEN

POETIC OFFS

RED HAPPENED

COIFFED FILE

DRAWER

UPROOTS NICE

Answers on page 178.

Call the Cops

ACROSS

1. Neighborhood cop, e.g.
5. Some luxury cars
8. Hit the sack
9. Slangy way to say "No!"
10. Annoyed state
11. "I Remember You" band
12. Cop, as an authority figure
14. Cop of the highway patrol
17. Uninterpreted info
19. Bible book before Philemon
21. Royal domain
22. Cop who's a detective
23. Used pencils, perhaps
24. Time of low temps

DOWN

1. Get steamy
2. Refinish, perhaps
3. "Animal Farm," e.g.
4. Most peculiar
6. Major responsibility for a parent
7. Draw back
9. Going to the dogs, e.g.
12. Blush
13. Theft deterrent
15. Where meals are made
16. Fluorescent pigment brand
18. Humpback, e.g.
19. Like a wallflower
20. 4-0 World Series win, e.g.

Track the Fugitive

The investigator is tracking the fugitive's past trips in order to find and recover information that was left behind in five cities. Each city was visited only once. Can you put together the travel timeline, using the information below?

1. Boston was not the third city visited.

2. The fugitive went north along the coastline immediately after visiting San Francisco.

3. Chicago was neither the first nor last city visited.

4. Seattle was visited sometime before Boston, but not immediately before.

5. Miami was visited sometime before Chicago, but not immediately before.

Answer on page 178.

DNA Sequence

Examine the two images below carefully. Are these sequences a match or not?

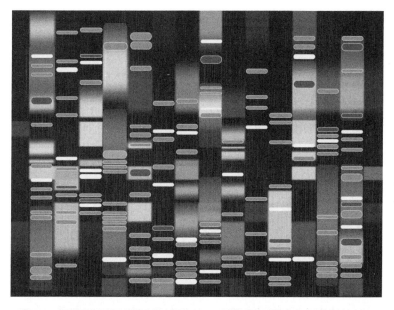

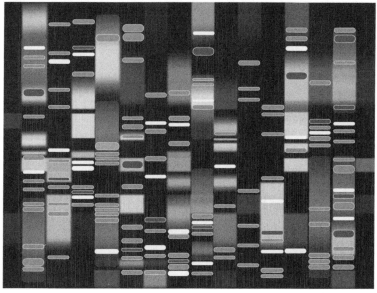

Answer on page 178.

Most Wanted Word Search

Every word listed is contained within the group of letters. Words can be found in a straight line horizontally, vertically, or diagonally. They may be read either forward or backward.

BUREAU	MOST WANTED
CAPTURE	POSTER
CRIME ALERT	PUBLIC
CRIMINAL	PUBLICITY
FEDERAL	REWARD
FUGITIVES	TEN
INVESTIGATION	WANTED
J. EDGAR HOOVER	WILLIAM HUTCHINSON

```
W I S T T I H Q V W P O S T E R I
S I O Q E K F U G I T I V E S I D
N P L I N A L B U R E A U X Z U M
C R H L F Z T I L R L T C M N A B
Z E H L I C I L B U P N P O S V X
A V H L W A O C Z E C J I P R V P
O O D G Y Z M A W T R T A T S A U
W O A E D D C H G C A U C Q W F B
G H D B T C Z A U G R R T A L R L
U R K R J N J C I T I I N P M U I
D A F Q A Z A T I M C T M L A F C
J G G B J W S W E L E H A I U C I
T D D Y Y E E A T D N R I C N O T
M E N T V H L R J S E P J N F A Y
A J Q N R E J L K D O A W J S W L
X G I N R H I A E M B M V E N O B
G I H T G M A F Y Y N K P P H Z N
```

How It All Began

Cryptograms are messages in substitution code. Break the code to read the message. For example, **THE SMART CAT** might become **FVO QWGDF JGF** if **F** is substituted for **T**, **V** for **H**, **O** for **E**, and so on.

TYEEYPF DYGLZV CONRCYGLHG TPL NCZ

ZQYNHK-YG-RCYZB BHK NCZ YGNZKGPNYHGPE

GZTL LZKSYRZ TCZG CZ CPQ P RHGSZKLPNYHG

TYNC A. ZQMPK CHHSZK. NCZ BXY NZG FHLN

TPGNZQ BOMYNYSZ EYLN TPL XHKG BKHF NCPN

QYLROLLYHG. VZPKL ZPKEYZK, CONRCYGLHG

CPQ PELH XZZG P KZIHKNZK PN NCZ BPFHOL

LRHIZL NKYPE.

Answer on page 179.

Overheard Information (Part I)

Read the story below, then turn the page and answer the questions.

While on a train, a bystander overheard a criminal tell an accomplice where a set of upcoming thefts would take place. The thief said, "On October 10 we hit the electronics store at Two Oaks Mall, the one on the second floor, not the one near the toy store. On October 12 we've got someone on the inside who will turn off the surveillance video at the jewelry store on the strip mall on 8th and Washington. Then we lie low for a week before hitting the bookstore on Western Avenue on October 20th."

Overheard Information (Part II)

(Do not read this until you have read the previous page!)

The bystander overheard the information about the crimes that were planned, but didn't have anywhere to write it down! Answer the questions below to help the bystander remember what to tell the police.

1. **The electronics store is found here.**
   - A. The first floor at Two Oaks Mall
   - B. The second floor at Two Oaks Mall
   - C. The strip mall on 8th and Washington
   - D. Western Avenue

2. **The thieves have an accomplice at this location.**
   - A. Electronics store
   - B. Jewelry store
   - C. Bookstore
   - D. There is no accomplice

3. **The bookstore is found on this street.**
   - A. Western Avenue
   - B. Western Drive
   - C. Western Court
   - D. Western Street

4. **The theft at the electronics place is scheduled for this day.**
   - A. October 10
   - B. October 12
   - C. October 14
   - D. October 20

Answers on page 179.

Seen at the Scene (Part I)

Study this picture of the crime scene for 1 minute, then turn the page.

Seen at the Scene (Part II)

(Do not read this until you have read the previous page!)

1. What were the numbers on the two evidence markers?

    A. 1 and 3

    B. 2 and 3

    C. 3 and 4

2. What is found at evidence marker 3?

    A. Bullet casing

    B. Flattened paper cup

    C. Shoe print

3. The investigator is wearing this.

    A. Jacket

    B. Sterile gown

    C. Poncho

Answers on page 179.

Motel Hideout

A thief hides out in one of the 45 motel rooms listed in the chart below. The motel's in-house detective received a sheet of four clues, signed "The Logical Thief." Using these clues, the detective found the room number within 15 minutes—but by that time, the thief had fled. Can you find the thief's motel room more quickly?

1. **The number either contains the digit 9, or the digits add up to 9.**
2. **If you multiply the two digits together, the result is not greater than 20 but greater than 10.**
3. **The number is not divisible by 5 or 6.**
4. **The number is not a cube number.**

51	52	53	54	55	56	57	58	59
41	42	43	44	45	46	47	48	49
31	32	33	34	35	36	37	38	39
21	22	23	24	25	26	27	28	29
11	12	13	14	15	16	17	18	19

Answer on page 179.

Find the Fugitive

Your location is marked by a dot. The fugitive's is marked by another. Can you track down the fugitive?

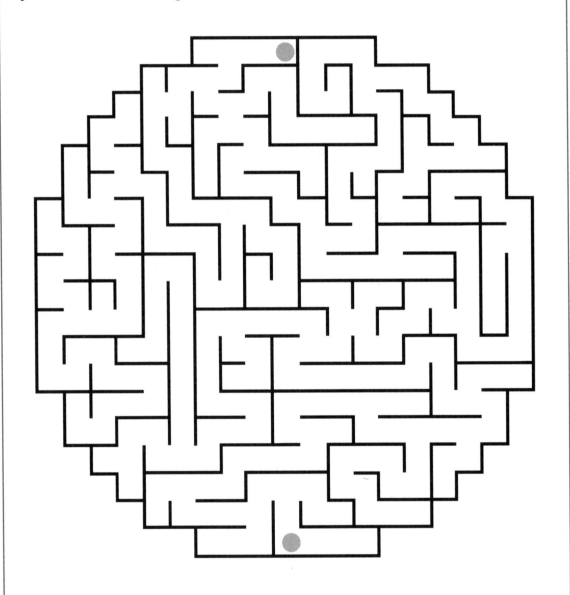

Answer on page 179.

Bank Robbery Alert (Part I)

A local bank was robbed! The bank has a poster up in its lobby, detailing what they know about the robbers. Read the page, then turn the page to answer questions.

Date: October 15, 2020

Time: 9:45 AM

Suspect description: Male, 6'1", race unknown, hair and eye color unknown

Wore blue vinyl gloves and a mask with red wig and a red mustache and beard attached

Weapon: Ruger LCP II

Getaway vehicle: rust-colored mid-size four-door sedan, possibly a Toyota, model unknown

License plates: Michigan plates, partial number 346 (final three digits)

Bank Robbery Alert (Part II)

(Do not read this until you have read the previous page!)

Fill in all the information you remember.

Date: _____

Time: _____

Suspect description: _____
_____
_____
_____

Weapon: _____

Getaway vehicle: _____
_____

License plates: _____

Answers on page 179.

Track the Fugitive

The investigator is tracking the fugitive's past trips in order to find and recover information that was left behind in five cities. Each city was visited only once. Can you put together the travel timeline, using the information below?

1. **From Paris, the fugitive went directly to the other capital city in Europe.**

2. **Seoul was not the last city visited.**

3. **Buenos Aires was visited sometime before, but not immediately before, Prague.**

4. **Cairo was one of the first three cities visited, but not the first.**

5. **From Asia, the fugitive went directly to South America.**

Answer on page 179.

Discover the Alias

The letters in the name ZOE can be found in boxes 4, 17, and 19, but not necessarily in that order. The same is true for the other names listed below. Using the names and the box numbers that follow each name as your guide, insert all the letters of the alphabet into the boxes. If you do this correctly, the shaded cells will reveal another name.

Hint: Look for words that share a single letter. For example, KATE shares only an **A** with LAURA and only an **E** with QUEENIE. By comparing the number lists following the names, you can deduce the box numbers of the shared letters.

BETH: 5, 7, 17, 25

BRENDA: 5, 15, 17, 18, 20, 23

CILLA: 21, 22, 23, 24

DAVINA: 15, 16, 20, 21, 23

FRANCES: 6, 10, 17, 18, 20, 22, 23

GLADYS: 6, 12, 14, 15, 23, 24

JOSIE: 1, 6, 17, 19, 21

KATE: 3, 17, 23, 25

LAURA: 13, 18, 23, 24

MARY: 14, 18, 23, 2a6

MAXINE: 2, 17, 20, 21, 23, 26

PATSY: 6, 11, 14, 23, 25

QUEENIE: 8, 13, 17, 20, 21

WANDA: 9, 15, 20, 23

ZOE: 4, 17, 19

1	2	3	4	5	6	7	8	9	10	11	12	13

14	15	16	17	18	19	20	21	22	23	24	25	26

Answers on page 179.

An Unwanted Record

Cryptograms are messages in substitution code. Break the code to read the message. For example, **THE SMART CAT** might become **FVO QWGDF JGF** if **F** is substituted for **T**, **V** for **H**, **O** for **E**, and so on.

RAWOIL EFHPQD ZQLQHF MJQHO 32 VQFLM

IH OXQ EIMO SFHOQG DAMO, DIHZQL

OXFH FHVIHQ QDMQ. OXIPZX XQ LQEFAHM

FO DFLZQ, XQ SFM LQEIRQG NLIE OXQ

DAMO AH 2016. XQ AM SFHOQG NIL FLEQG

LIUUQLV IN F SQDDM NFLZI GQJIO.

Answer on page 180.

Baddies of Fiction

ACROSS

1. Hot rocks
5. Boggy land
8. Belch, say
12. "Deliver us from ___"
13. "Do the Right Thing" director
14. Hip-hop trio Salt-N-___
15. Count calories
16. Archer's wood
17. Arrogant sort
18. "The Demon Barber of Fleet Street"
21. 1985 Kurosawa classic
22. A in German class?
23. Coal worker
26. "The Big Bang Theory" character from India
27. Barrel at a bash
30. "Nightmare on Elm Street" villain
33. It's often left hanging
34. A pal of Pooh
35. Easy gait
36. Big embrace
37. "Fifth Beatle" Yoko
38. "Psycho" weirdo
43. Sonny or Chastity
44. "___ culpa"
45. "Don't worry about me"
47. Orders a dog to attack

48. Escort's offering
49. 1980s Dodge model
50. "Iliad" war god
51. "___ Skylark" (Shelley)
52. Apollo acronym

DOWN

1. Blazed a trail
2. Alamo alternative
3. Panoramic sight
4. Did a tailoring job
5. Robin Hood portrayer Errol
6. Bigfoot's shoe size?
7. It begins in January
8. Big name in printers
9. Fix, as socks
10. It can help you carry a tune
11. Eatery check
19. Body part that vibrates
20. Baja border city
23. Artist's degree
24. Abbr. on a clothing reject tag
25. Hoop hanger
26. "King Kong" and "Citizen Kane" studio
27. C.I.A.'s Soviet counterpart
28. Aquarium wriggler
29. College sr.'s exam
31. Something to meditate on
32. Feeling
36. 1990s candidate ___ Perot

37. 2009 Peace Prize   Nobelist
38. "Film ___" (dark movie
    genre)
39. "The Raven" start
40. "Fiddling" emperor

41. Madame Bovary
42. Heirs, often
43. "Be prepared" org.
46. Cadenza maker

Track the Fugitive

The investigator is tracking the fugitive's past trips in order to find and recover information that was left behind in five cities. Each city was visited only once. Can you put together the travel timeline, using the information below?

1. **The fugitive went from Denver directly to New Orleans.**

2. **The fugitive did not go from New Orleans to either Indianapolis or Portland.**

3. **Hartford was not the last city on the fugitive's list.**

4. **The fugitive went to Indianapolis before Portland, but not immediately before.**

Answer on page 180.

Examine the two images below carefully. Are these sequences a match or not?

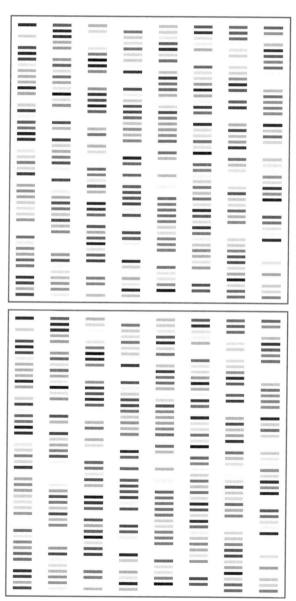

Cryptograms are messages in substitution code. Break the code to read the message. For example, **THE SMART CAT** might become **FVO QWGDF JGF** if **F** is substituted for **T**, **V** for **H**, **O** for **E**, and so on.

ZDGGDQ SROPDI ZNWSIP OLQIP CSNJGW SIW

PDHQ KI PCQ HKOP USIPQJ GDOP, SZKRP PUK

CKRNO. ZNWSIP, UCK CSJ QOXSLQJ ANKH

LNDOKI DI 1968, NKZZQJ S ZSIF DI 1969, PCQI

OCKP SIJ FDGGQJ PUK AZD SBQIPO UCK UQNQ

OQIP PK XSLPRNQ CDH. CQ USO LGSXQJ KI PCQ

HKOP USIPQJ GDOP AKN PCKOQ HRNJQNO, ZRP

USO SLLNQCQIJQJ PCSP OSHQ JSW.

Answer on page 180.

Track the Fugitive

The investigator is tracking the fugitive's past trips in order to find and recover information that was left behind in five cities. Each city was visited only once. Can you put together the travel timeline, using the information below?

1. **The fugitive neither began nor ended his journey in Johannesburg.**

2. **Rio de Janeiro was visited either immediately before or immediately after New York.**

3. **Law enforcement almost caught the fugitive in Jakarta, but he took the first flight out to Perth.**

4. **Johannesburg was visited sometime after Perth.**

5. **From South Africa, the fugitive went immediately to South America.**

Answer on page 180.

Richard Miller

Every word in all capitals below is contained within the group of letters. Words can be found in a straight line horizontally, vertically, or diagonally. They may be read either forward or backward.

Richard **MILLER** was an **FBI AGENT** with a **SHODDY** track **RECORD**, criticized for being **UNKEMPT** and taking long **LUNCHES** rather than working. He was **ALSO** selling **CLASSIFIED** information to the **RUSSIANS**. Miller had an **AFFAIR** with a married woman named **SVETLANA** Ogorodnikov. Richard, Svetlana, and Svetlana's **HUSBAND** Nikolai were all **ARRESTED** in 1984 for **WORKING** with the **KGB**. Miller served **THREE** years of a longer **SENTENCE**.

```
L U N C H E S O G D M T H R E E
T K A N A L T E V S R G V U J P
H J N I Q H Q U S I I O N N A Z
V P T L W E U U Q B X K C G K X
L W F Q C H M S F U E T E E S U
Z D E D L L O N B M S N V N R N
E F E U A S D J P A T F A K G M
G Z V T S A E T C X N I A Y G P
G G F Q S B N N R R S D L Q Y B
T W M C I E T X T S C O S W W S
Y Y I G F L R A U E M E O I F B
P D L G I H P R F G N R K A O L
R D L F E M Z J A F K C K E K K
M O E F D E E A B I A U E K F T
Z H R O B W I R N S X I D Z T R
Y S C Z A Y M G F Z U H R N B G
```

Motel Hideout

A thief hides out in one of the 45 motel rooms listed in the chart below. The motel's in-house detective received a sheet of four clues, signed "The Logical Thief." Using these clues, the detective found the room number within 15 minutes—but by that time, the thief had fled. Can you find the thief's motel room more quickly?

1. **The number does not have the digit 3 in it.**
2. **The digits do not add up to 10.**
3. **The number is even.**
4. **Add 5 to the first digit to get the second digit.**

51	52	53	54	55	56	57	58	59
41	42	43	44	45	46	47	48	49
31	32	33	34	35	36	37	38	39
21	22	23	24	25	26	27	28	29
11	12	13	14	15	16	17	18	19

Answer on page 180.

Cryptograms are messages in substitution code. Break the code to read the message. For example, **THE SMART CAT** might become **FVO QWGDF JGF** if **F** is substituted for **T**, **V** for **H**, **O** for **E**, and so on.

HMZFZGBEN BMP GIO MBGCPJ IG OXP RDZ

FINO TBGOPJ EZNO. GIO IGEW OXBO, DQO

OXPMP XBSP NIFPOZFPN DPPG FIMP OXBG OPG

ZGJZSZJQBEN IG OXP EZNO.

Park Pursuit

Can you escape pursuit and flee the park?

Answer on page 181.

The Fugitive Ran and Hid

Change just one letter on each line to go from the top word to the bottom word. Do not change the order of the letters. You must have a common English word at each step.

RAN

‾‾‾‾‾‾

‾‾‾‾‾‾

‾‾‾‾‾‾

HID

Find the Criminal

LOOK

‾‾‾‾‾‾

‾‾‾‾‾‾

‾‾‾‾‾‾

‾‾‾‾‾‾

FIND

Answers on page 181.

Crime Anagrams

Unscramble each word or phrase below to reveal a word or phrase of a crime.

DANK PIPING

BARBERRY DOME

CHAT FRET

AGATE SOB

ROTE TOXIN

ECZEMA GRIDIRON

KIT GRUFF CARDING

MOBBING

Answers on page 181.

Overheard Information (Part I)

Read the story below, then turn the page and answer the questions.

While on a train, a bystander overheard a criminal tell an accomplice where a set of upcoming thefts would take place. The criminal said, "We're hitting up a bunch of stores on August 12, or August 19 if we do get that heat wave. But if it's under 100, we're still on. This is the order: first the tea shop on Rivers Street, then go to Bakers Avenue for the toy store. Then we ditch the loot at the safehouse on Third Street before going across town to Secondhand Wonders on Fifth Street before going to ground."

Overheard Information (Part II)

(Do not read this until you have read the previous page!)

The bystander overheard the information about the crimes that were planned, but didn't have anywhere to write it down! Answer the questions below to help the bystander remember what to tell the police.

1. The first location will be:

      A. A tea shop

      B. A toy store

      C. A resale shop

      D. An electronics store

2. If there is a heat wave, the thefts will take place on this day.

      A. August 12

      B. August 15

      C. August 17

      D. August 19

3. The safehouse is found on this street.

      A. Rivers Street

      B. Bakers Street

      C. Bakers Avenue

      D. Third Street

4. The resale shop is named:

      A. Secondhand Treasures

      B. Secondhand Wonders

      C. Secondhand Resale

      D. Vintage Treasures

Answers on page 181.

The investigator is tracking the fugitive's past trips in order to find and recover information that was left behind in five cities. Each city was visited only once. Can you put together the travel timeline, using the information below?

1. **The two Great Lakes cities were not visited one after the other.**

2. **Atlanta was either the first or last city visited.**

3. **Chicago was visited sometime after Pittsburgh.**

4. **From Milwaukee, the fugitive went directly to the city in Florida.**

5. **Tampa was visited sometime before Pittsburgh.**

6. **At least one other city separates the visits between Atlanta and Chicago.**

Answer on page 181.

Most Wanted Stats

Cryptograms are messages in substitution code. Break the code to read the message. For example, **THE SMART CAT** might become **FVO QWGDF JGF** if **F** is substituted for **T**, **V** for **H**, **O** for **E**, and so on.

EHLG OWXF 500 IGHIDG WXRG TGGF ZFPDQJGJ

HF OWG DZMO. SWZDG EHLG OWXF 90 IGLPGFO

HC OWHMG DZMOGJ WXRG TGGF PXQNWO,

HFDV XTHQO 160 SGLG PXQNWO TGPXQMG HC

OZIM CLHE OWG IQTDZP.

Answer on page 181.

Examine the two images below carefully. Are these sequences a match or not?

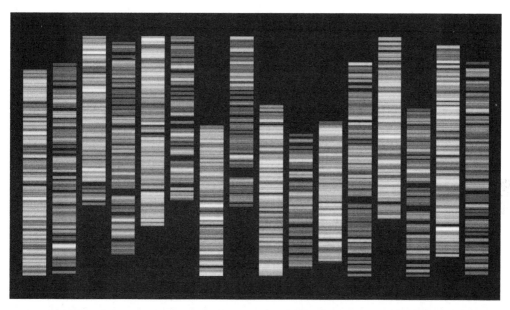

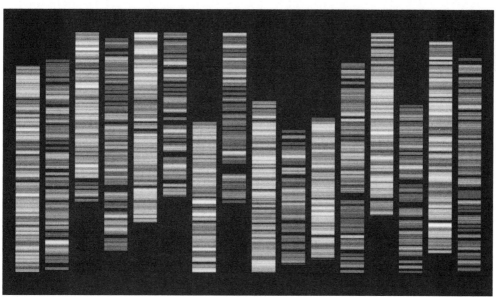

Motel Hideout

A thief hides out in one of the 45 motel rooms listed in the chart below. The motel's in-house detective received a sheet of four clues, signed "The Logical Thief." Using these clues, the detective found the room number within 15 minutes—but by that time, the thief had fled. Can you find the thief's motel room more quickly?

1. **The sum of the digits is greater than 8.**
2. **If you multiply the digits, the resulting number is greater than 25.**
3. **The number is not prime.**
4. **The number is a square number.**

51	52	53	54	55	56	57	58	59
41	42	43	44	45	46	47	48	49
31	32	33	34	35	36	37	38	39
21	22	23	24	25	26	27	28	29
11	12	13	14	15	16	17	18	19

Answer on page 181.

Track the Fugitive

The investigator is tracking the fugitive's past trips in order to find and recover information that was left behind in five cities. Each city was visited only once. Can you put together the travel timeline, using the information below?

1. **From Philadelphia, the fugitive went to a Midwestern city.**

2. **The fugitive did not go to Charleston last.**

3. **The fugitive's first spot was either Omaha or San Jose.**

4. **The fugitive went to Boston sometime before Philadelphia.**

5. **At least one city separated the trip from San Jose and the trip to Charleston.**

Discover the Alias

The letters in the name BILL can be found in boxes 2, 8, and 18, but not necessarily in that order. The same is true for the other men's names listed below. Using the names and the box numbers that follow them to guide you, insert all the letters of the alphabet into the boxes. If you do this correctly, the shaded cells will reveal 2 more names.

Hint: Look for words that share a single letter. For example, PAUL shares only a **P** with STEPHEN and only an **A** with MAX. By comparing the number lists following those 2 names, you can deduce the box numbers of those shared letters.

BILL: 2, 8, 18

CARL: 4, 6, 7, 8

DAVID: 2, 6, 16, 26

FRED: 7, 9, 12, 16

GREGORY: 7, 9, 22, 24, 25

JOHN: 3, 5, 22, 23

JIM: 2, 3, 14

MARK: 6, 7, 14, 19

MAX: 6, 14, 15

PAUL: 1, 6, 8, 11

QUENTIN: 2, 9, 11, 17, 21, 23

ROWAN: 6, 7, 13, 22, 23

STEPHEN: 1, 5, 9, 10, 21, 23

ZAK: 6, 19, 20

1	2	3	4	5	6	7	8	9	10	11	12	13

14	15	16	17	18	19	20	21	22	23	24	25	26

Answers on page 181.

Not a Ruthless Crime?

Cryptograms are messages in substitution code. Break the code to read the message. For example, **THE SMART CAT** might become **FVO QWGDF JGF** if **F** is substituted for **T**, **V** for **H**, **O** for **E**, and so on.

MQOT JYNJEBFF-NWTYJM BFZ TJM PHVKMYJFZ

CYZFBIIJZ OTJ ZBQGTOJM HK B SJBDOTV MJBD

JNOBOJ ZJRJDHIJM KHM MBFNHE YF 1968.

STYDJ TJM PHVKMYJFZ SBN WBQGTO YF NTHMO

HMZJM, MQOT JNWBIJZ WBIOQMJ KHM BDEHNO

OTMJJ EHFOTN. NTJ SBN OTJ KYMNO SHEBF

IDBWJZ HF OTJ EHNO SBFOJZ DYNO.

Track the Fugitive

The investigator is tracking the fugitive's past trips in order to find and recover information that was left behind in five cities. Each city was visited only once. Can you put together the travel timeline, using the information below?

1. **The visit to Mexico City came direclty between the visits to the two Canadian cities.**

2. **Copenhagen was one of the first two cities visited.**

3. **Ottawa was visited immediately before the other city that began with O.**

4. **Toronto was visited sometime before Oslo.**

Answer on page 182.

The First of Seventeen

Cryptograms are messages in substitution code. Break the code to read the message. For example, **THE SMART CAT** might become **FVO QWGDF JGF** if **F** is substituted for **T**, **V** for **H**, **O** for **E**, and so on.

PWU ZEA IMUOAPN PWU NWHT "SFUMAIS'N

FHNP TSGPUO" TAPW DUSOAGK PH PWU

ISJPQMU HZ NURUGPUUG ZQKAPARUN. PWU

RUMX ZAMNP UJANHOU MUNQDPUO AG

RAUTUM PAJN PWSP EMHQKWP SEHQP PWU

ISJPQMU HZ OSRAO BSFUN MHEUMPN.

Find the Fugitive

Chase the fleeing fugitive before she gets to the top of the building and escapes by helicopter!

Answer on page 182.

You've intercepted a message between a criminal who fled and his accomplice. But the message doesn't seem to make sense! Can you discover the criminal's current location hidden in the message?

MOM WE SEE IT
THEM TOO THEN DANCED EXTRA SILLY
FEAR TO GOING SEE KIDNAPPER BOSS
VIP AREA NEAR PADLOCK

Donnie Brasco

Every word in all capitals below is contained within the group of letters. Words can be found in a straight line horizontally, vertically, or diagonally. They may be read either forward or backward.

The movie "DONNIE Brasco," starring Johnny DEPP in the title ROLE, tells the STORY of an UNDERCOVER agent from the FBI who INFILTRATES a CRIME family. BRASCO gains the CONFIDENCE of GANGSTER Lefty RUGGIERO (Al PACINO) while POSING as a JEWEL thief.

The MOVIE was based on REAL life EVENTS. Brasco was the undercover ALIAS of JOSEPH Dominick PISTONE. He infiltrated the BONANNO and COLOMBO crime families, two of the FIVE FAMILIES of New YORK City's MAFIA. Brasco took GEMOLOGY courses BEFORE going undercover as a jewel THIEF.

```
S S R O L E I N N O D Y L A R O
T T E Y E C N E D I F N O C X B
N N G T J R Y B R A S C O O M M
E S I Y A I U J S U P C M A Y O
V A D G G R B G E P G A R E Z L
E I A N T O T F I W K G C I F O
I L U I C I L L G E N I I M C
D A N S I W L O I D A L V E N E
J D D O N T A B M F V N O K R O
O A E P M L I E A E N X S Y G O
S T R P P A F F F Y G I O T M A
E H C F P E A O E T L R I W E R
P I O W I R M R V R K Y Z O J R
H E V I U I W E I E Y R O T S S
X F E E I V O M F B O N A N N O
O H R N E N O T S I P H Y H M M
```

Track the Fugitive

The investigator is tracking the fugitive's past trips in order to find and recover information that was left behind in five cities. Each city was visited only once. Can you put together the travel timeline, using the information below?

1. **The fugitive went from Stockholm directly to the capital of Liechtenstein.**

2. **Vienna and the other city that started with V were neither the first nor last cities.**

3. **Paris was either the first or fourth city.**

4. **The trip to Berlin was preceded immediately by a trip to Vaduz.**

Answer on page 182.

Seen at the Scene (Part I)

Study this picture of the crime scene for 1 minute, then turn the page.

Seen at the Scene (Part II)

(Do not read this until you have read the previous page!)

1. What does the investigator hold in his right hand?

    A. Magnifying glass

    B. Tweezers

    C. Camera

2. What is on the ground to the right of the investigator?

    A. Gun

    B. Tweezers

    C. Camera

3. The ground is made of this kind of material.

    A. Grass

    B. Gravel

    C. Cement / concrete

Answers on page 182.

Motel Hideout

A thief hides out in one of the 45 motel rooms listed in the chart below. The motel's in-house detective received a sheet of four clues, signed "The Logical Thief." Using these clues, the detective found the room number within 15 minutes—but by that time, the thief had fled. Can you find the thief's motel room more quickly?

1. **The number is odd.**
2. **The number is not a multiple of 3, nor does it have 3 as one of the digits.**
3. **The number is prime.**
4. **The sum of the digits is less than 5**

51	52	53	54	55	56	57	58	59
41	42	43	44	45	46	47	48	49
31	32	33	34	35	36	37	38	39
21	22	23	24	25	26	27	28	29
11	12	13	14	15	16	17	18	19

Answer on page 182.

Track the Fugitive

The investigator is tracking the fugitive's past trips in order to find and recover information that was left behind in five cities. Each city was visited only once. Can you put together the travel timeline, using the information below?

1. **From Cape Town, the fugitive fled to either Pretoria or Gabarone.**

2. **Dakar was not one of the first two cities visited.**

3. **Gabarone was visited immediately before Nairobi.**

4. **At least one other city separated the visits to Cape Town and Dakar.**

5. **Nairobi was visited sometime after Dakar, but not immediately afterward.**

Answer on page 182.

A Scary Partnership

Cryptograms are messages in substitution code. Break the code to read the message. For example, **THE SMART CAT** might become **FVO QWGDF JGF** if **F** is substituted for **T**, **V** for **H**, **O** for **E**, and so on.

LJFCQK NQCWK JFBZWD QDZ YIQDOEK

AWQLEDX SWIW IWKGFDKEPBW YFI

LJW JFBZWD-AWQLEDX XQDX FY QICWZ

IFPPWIEWK. LFXWLJWI, QBFDX SELJ RQIEFMK

QOOFCGBEOWK, LJWU IFPPWZ LIQEDK, PQDAK,

QDZ Q M.K. CQEB LIMOA.

The Fugitive Flees to France

The letters in BRIGITTE can be found in boxes 3, 4, 5, 6, 7, and 23 but not necessarily in that order. Similarly, the letters in the other names of French women can be found in the boxes indicated. Your task is to insert all the letters of the alphabet into the boxes. If you do this correctly, the shaded cells will reveal another French female name.

Hint: Compare YVONNE AND YVETTE to get the value of T, then YVETTE and VALERIE for the value of Y.

Unused letters: K, W, and X

BRIGITTE: 3, 4, 5, 6, 7, 23

CLAUDETTE: 2, 5, 7, 9, 12, 14, 15

FRANCOISE: 2, 3, 4, 5, 10, 11, 15, 16, 20

GISELLE: 4, 5, 10, 12, 23

HELENE: 5, 12, 20, 22

JACQUELINE: 2, 4, 5, 9, 12, 13, 15, 19, 20

JEANNE: 2, 5, 13, 20

MONIQUE: 1, 4, 5, 9, 11, 19, 20

PAULETTE: 2, 5, 7, 9, 12, 21

SIMONE: 1, 4, 5, 10, 11, 20

SOPHIE: 4, 5, 10, 11, 21, 22

SUZETTE: 5, 7, 8, 9, 10

VALERIE: 2, 3, 4, 5, 12, 18

YVETTE: 5, 7, 17, 18

YVONNE: 5, 11, 17, 18, 20

1	2	3	4	5	6	7	8	9	10	11	12	13

14	15	16	17	18	19	20	21	22	23	24	25	26
										K	W	X

Answers on page 183.

Overheard Information (Part I)

Read the story below, then turn the page and answer the questions.

While on a train, a bystander overheard a woman tell a thief about how best to rob an office. The woman said, "First, you have to promise not to steal any personal stuff from people, just the office stuff. Except from the Director of Marketing, you can take anything from her office, she's mean. They just got new computers for the Sales department, really nice laptops, and those are in the South wing. The CEO has a safe in his office, behind the Monet poster, and the combination is 62-13-21."

Overheard Information (Part II)

(Do not read this until you have read the previous page!)

The bystander overheard the information about the crimes that were planned, but didn't have anywhere to write it down! Answer the questions below to help the bystander remember what to tell the police.

1. The woman urges the man to steal from this person specifically.

    A. Director of Marketing

    B. Director of Sales

    C. Director of IT

    D. The CEO

2. The newest laptops on the building are found in this wing.

    A. North

    B. South

    C. East

    D. West

3. The safe is found here.

    A. In the CEO's office, underneath his desk

    B. In the CEO's office, behind a painting

    C. In the CEO's office, behind a poster by Monet

    D. In the CEO's office, behind a poster by Manet

4. This is the combination for the safe.

    A. 62-13-21

    B. 62-21-13

    C. 62-31-21

    D. 62-13-12

Answers on page 183.

Cryptograms are messages in substitution code. Break the code to read the message. For example, **THE SMART CAT** might become **FVO QWGDF JGF** if **F** is substituted for **T**, **V** for **H**, **O** for **E**, and so on.

H WKQJA NBGHPDSB KY VHSW RNKRFBPP CHV

PCB OHIB JHIB HO CDO YHIKQO NBGHPDKJ,

ZQP THO HJ KQPGHT. CB BORHLBV EQOPDRB DJ

1872, YGBBDJA PK H NHJRC.

DNA Sequence

Examine the two images below carefully. Are these sequences a match or not?

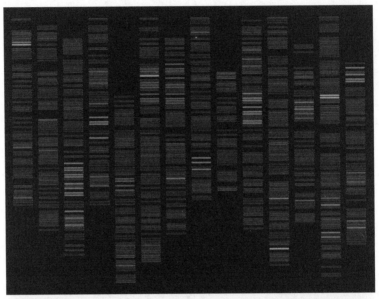

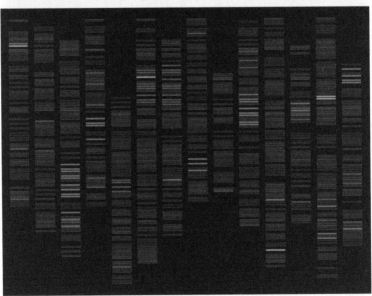

Answer on page 183.

Not Quite a Wanted Poster

Cryptograms are messages in substitution code. Break the code to read the message. For example, **THE SMART CAT** might become **FVO QWGDF JGF** if **F** is substituted for **T**, **V** for **H**, **O** for **E**, and so on.

UZNLFH ULI GSV XLIIFKGRLM RM SRH

KLORGRXZO NZXSRMV, DROORZN "YLHH"

GDVVW UOVW GL HKZRM DSROV LM SLFHV

ZIIVHG. SV DZH XZFTSG YVXZFHV HLNVLMV

GSVIV IVXLTMRAVW SRN WFV GL KLORGRXZO

XZIGLLMH GSZG HPVDVIVW SRH XLIIFKG

"GZNNZMB SZOO" NZXSRMV.

Motel Hideout

A thief hides out in one of the 45 motel rooms listed in the chart below. The motel's in-house detective received a sheet of four clues, signed "The Logical Thief." Using these clues, the detective found the room number within 15 minutes—but by that time, the thief had fled. Can you find the thief's motel room more quickly?

1. **The number is a multiple of 4.**
2. **The number is not a multiple of 3.**
3. **The first digit is larger than the second digit.**
4. **The sum of the digits is 1 less than when you multiply the digits.**

51	52	53	54	55	56	57	58	59
41	42	43	44	45	46	47	48	49
31	32	33	34	35	36	37	38	39
21	22	23	24	25	26	27	28	29
11	12	13	14	15	16	17	18	19

Answer on page 183.

Track the Fugitive

The investigator is tracking the fugitive's past trips in order to find and recover information that was left behind in five cities. Each city was visited only once. Can you put together the travel timeline, using the information below?

1. From Seoul the fugitive went immediately to Tokyo or vice versa.

2. The fugitive did not go to or from the other U.S. city from Los Angeles.

3. Barcelona was visited sometime before New York, but not immediately before.

4. Los Angeles was visited sometime before Tokyo.

5. Two other cities separated the visit to Barcelona and the visit to Tokyo.

Answer on page 183.

Heist Movies

ACROSS

1. 1995 De Niro/Pacino heist movie
5. Brought up, as a child
11. 11th century Spanish hero
13. Hindu drink of immortality
14. "Sweetheart" of "Jersey Shore"
15. Inuit in a 1922 film classic
16. 2008 Jason Statham heist movie
18. "Others" in a Latin phrase
19. Canadian satirist Mort
22. "The ___ Job," 2003 Mark Wahlberg heist movie
25. Culpa preceder
26. Cow's first stomach
27. Convocation of witches
29. Aladdin's monkey pal
30. 1964 Melina Mercouri heist movie
32. Backtalk
34. "That's not ___!" (parent's warning)
35. 1999 Connery/Zeta- Jones heist movie
40. Samantha's mother on "Bewitched"
42. Grammy-winning country star Steve
43. Women's ___ (feminist)
44. Fencing foils
45. Arctic waters, on historical maps
46. Galahad and Lancelot, e.g.

DOWN

1. Command, of yore
2. David and Goliath's battlefield
3. Highest point
4. Pastry shell filled with meat, fish, etc.
5. First elected Congresswoman Jeannette
6. Key of Billy Joel's "Uptown Girl": Abbr.
7. Works by New Yorker cartoonist Peter
8. City in central Ecuador
9. DDE's WWII command
10. Deadwood's terr.
12. Call a radio show, say
17. Actress Long or Peeples
20. Big pile
21. Notes between sol and do
22. 401(k) alternatives
23. Big brass horn
24. Getting a charge out of
27. Epic poem
28. Celestial diagrams
30. Lead-in to "boom-de-ay"
31. Wireless communication: Abbr.
33. Stuck-up types
36. Maple or cherry
37. "Able was I ___ saw Elba"
38. Atlanta Brave or New York Met, slangily
39. Trueheart of "Dick Tracy"

40. Yale booster
41. Actor Cage, to friends

Murder in Utah

Cryptograms are messages in substitution code. Break the code to read the message. For example, **THE SMART CAT** might become **FVO QWGDF JGF** if **F** is substituted for **T**, **V** for **H**, **O** for **E**, and so on.

KOPJBCQ AZOIPJJ UPQ P MPQRLO—PJV P

ISOVZOZO. HLOJ BCOBP 1850, AZ ILTZV RL

RAZ SJCRZV QRPRZQ KOLI ZJGFPJV. ACQ

KCOQR RUL UCTZQ VCZV SJVZO QSQMCBCLSQ

BCOBSIQRPJBZQ. AZOIPJJ FPRZO ISOVZOZV

RUL ULIZJ CJ QPFR FPEZ BCRX. JLR FLJG PKRZO

RAZCO VZPRAQ, AZ KFZV QPFR FPEZ BCRX PJV

ZQBPMZV DSQRCBZ, ZTPVCJG BPMRSOZ.

Answer on page 183.

Motel Hideout

A thief hides out in one of the 45 motel rooms listed in the chart below. The motel's in-house detective received a sheet of four clues, signed "The Logical Thief." Using these clues, the detective found the room number within 15 minutes—but by that time, the thief had fled. Can you find the thief's motel room more quickly?

1. **The number is not prime.**
2. **Neither digit is a prime number (note that the smallest prime number is 2).**
3. **The number is not divisible by 4 or 7.**
4. **The number is divisible by 6.**

51	52	53	54	55	56	57	58	59
41	42	43	44	45	46	47	48	49
31	32	33	34	35	36	37	38	39
21	22	23	24	25	26	27	28	29
11	12	13	14	15	16	17	18	19

Answer on page 183.

Public Enemy #1: Alvin Karpis

Every word in all capitals below is contained within the group of letters. Words can be found in a straight line horizontally, vertically, or diagonally. They may be read either forward or backward.

ALVIN Karpis aka "CREEPY" Karpis, was a GANGSTER in the 1930s. He led the Barker-KARPIS Gang with the BARKER brothers. Karpis was DESIGNATED Public ENEMY #1 by the FBI.

BORN in CANADA in 1907, Karpis was RAISED in KANSAS. He was first IMPRISONED in 1926 for attempted BURGLARY but made an ESCAPE. He was later caught for CAR theft and was PUT in the Kansas State PENITENTIARY, where he met FRED Barker. After their RELEASE, they joined FORCES in a RUTHLESS gang that even DARED to KILL a SHERIFF.

Karpis was eventually CAUGHT and sent to ALCATRAZ, where he SERVED 26 years before being put on PAROLE. He died in SPAIN in 1979.

```
Z  G  R  U  T  H  L  E  S  S  R  A  C  Y  A  K
U  E  P  O  D  E  S  I  A  R  N  S  I  C  D  E
F  U  R  H  U  X  K  P  I  A  U  E  M  K  A  N
T  B  V  Y  R  A  K  B  E  N  L  R  P  Y  N  E
Y  P  I  L  N  I  A  P  S  U  E  V  R  E  A  M
R  D  E  S  I  G  N  A  T  E  D  E  I  Y  C  Y
A  Z  A  R  T  A  C  L  A  Z  B  D  S  N  B  R
I  S  E  E  D  S  I  P  R  A  K  F  O  P  G  A
T  R  I  L  J  V  A  L  R  R  U  F  N  A  B  L
N  T  I  E  C  N  Y  K  Q  E  K  I  E  R  T  G
E  A  C  A  D  P  E  T  S  T  S  R  D  O  X  R
T  P  D  S  E  R  T  X  H  S  A  E  M  L  D  U
I  B  A  E  L  L  I  K  E  G  P  H  C  E  N  B
N  T  R  C  R  Z  S  L  S  N  U  S  R  R  A  R
E  C  R  A  S  F  A  P  E  A  H  A  O  G  O  H
P  D  Z  A  U  E  D  V  E  G  D  B  C  J  U  F
```

Answers on page 184.

A Trusty Fellow

Cryptograms are messages in substitution code. Break the code to read the message. For example, **THE SMART CAT** might become **FVO QWGDF JGF** if **F** is substituted for **T**, **V** for **H**, **O** for **E**, and so on.

SWCCWRD FIMBWN, BGLF WF 1899 WF WGSR,

TLIS PJ NG BIEGDI R ZISIC NXWIO (RFH R

DPLHILIL, RONIL XI AWCCIH R OICCGS NXWIO).

WDJLWMGFIH, XI BIERDI R EXRPOOIPL NG NXI

SRLHIF. XI PMIH XWM LICRNWQI OLIIHGD NG

IMERJI OLGD JLWMGF WF 1946. XI SRM GFI

GO NXI OWLMN IFNLRFNM GF NXI OBW DGMN

SRFNIH CWMN, RFH SRM LIERJNPLIH WF 1950.

Answer on page 184.

Catch the Suspect

Can you find the only path to track the fugitive?

Change just one letter on each line to go from the top word to the bottom word. Do not change the order of the letters. Unless the clue indicates otherwise, you must have a common English word at each step.

FLED

_____

_____

_____

_____

_____

_____ **The Greek god of war**

AREA

Answers on page 184.

Unscramble each word or phrase below to reveal a word or phrase related to the FIB...er, FBI.

GET AN

OVERHEARD JOG

CLEANER MEW FONT

ICED TOMS

TELLING NIECE

IT IRIS JOCUND

NO ACQUIT

ANY SALT

Track the Fugitive

The investigator is tracking the fugitive's past trips in order to find and recover information that was left behind in five cities. Each city was visited only once. Can you put together the travel timeline, using the information below?

1. **The fugitive began in either Rome or Florence.**

2. **The fugitive's final visit was to either Florence or Naples.**

3. **The fugitive went to Milan before Palermo, but not immediately before.**

4. **The fugitive did not go from Palermo to Naples.**

Answer on page 184.

Bank Robbery Alert (Part I)

A local bank was robbed! The bank has a poster up in its lobby, detailing what they know about the robbers. Read the page, then turn the page to answer questions.

Date: January 8, 2021

Time: 2:17 to 2:33 PM

Suspect description:

White male, 5'10", short brown hair, eye color unknown, wore a mask over the lower part of his face

White female, 5'5", shoulder-length layered brown hair, eye color unknown, wore sunglasses and a mask over the lower part of her face

A third suspect, description unknown, drove the getaway vehicle

Names: Male robber referred to woman as "Darling" and "Sweet Lily"

Weapons: Machine guns

Getaway vehicle: small-size SUV, black, license plates unknown

Bank Robbery Alert (Part II)

(Do not read this until you have read the previous page!)

Fill in all the information you remember.

Date: _____

Time: _____

Suspect descriptions:

Suspect 1:

_____

_____

_____

_____

Suspect 2:

_____

_____

_____

_____

Suspect 3:

_____

_____

_____

_____

Names: _____

Weapons: _____

Getaway vehicle: _____

Answers on page 184.

Where's the Fugitive?

The letters in CAPE COT COTTAGE can be found in boxes 1, 3, 4, 5, 11, 13, 15, and 22, but not necessarily in that order. Similarly, the letters in all these words can be found in the boxes indicated. Your task is to insert all the letters of the alphabet into the boxes. If you do this correctly, the shaded cells will reveal another word.

Hint: Compare PUP TENT and HUNTING LODGE to get the value of P, then PUP TENT to WHITE HOUSE to get the value of N.

Unused letters: J, X, and Z

CAPE COD COTTAGE 1, 3, 4, 5, 11, 13, 15, 22

COUNTRY VILLA 1, 3, 7, 8, 9, 10, 11, 13, 14, 20, 21

CRASH PAD 1, 4, 6, 10, 13, 15, 16

DUDE RANCH 1, 4, 5, 9, 10, 13, 14, 16

GRASS SHACK 1, 6, 10, 13, 16, 19, 22

HOLIDAY INN 1, 3, 4, 7, 8, 14, 16, 20

HUNTING LODGE 3, 4, 5, 7, 9, 11, 14, 16, 20, 22

LOG CABIN 1, 2, 3, 7, 13, 14, 20, 22

MOTOR HOME 3, 5, 10, 11, 16, 17

PUP TENT 5, 9, 11, 14, 15

QUONSET HUT 3, 5, 6, 9, 11, 14, 16, 23

SKI CHALET 1, 5, 6, 7, 11, 13, 16, 19, 20

TRUCK FARM 1, 9, 10, 11, 12, 13, 17, 19

WHITE HOUSE 3, 4, 5, 6, 7, 9, 11, 16, 18

1	2	3	4	5	6	7	8	9	10	11	12	13

14	15	16	17	18	19	20	21	22	23	24	25	26
										J	X	Z

A Short Time Free

Cryptograms are messages in substitution code. Break the code to read the message. For example, **THE SMART CAT** might become **FVO QWGDF JGF** if **F** is substituted for **T**, **V** for **H**, **O** for **E**, and so on.

DF TDN XHSFJQL YOXN, PQF JHCYQF EGGHCCSE

VON O POFB LHPPQL OFY QNGOIQY ILDNHFQL.

IOLHCQY DF 1961 OMRQL O NRDFR DF ILDNHF,

TQ YDQY DF 1963—RTQ UDGRDE HM PSLJCOLN

VTH QFRQLQY TDN THEQ.

Answer on page 184.

Track the Fugitive

The investigator is tracking the fugitive's past trips in order to find and recover information that was left behind in five cities. Each city was visited only once. Can you put together the travel timeline, using the information below?

1. **London was the first, third, or fifth city visited.**

2. **The city in Wales was visited before the city in Scotland, but not immediately before.**

3. **Neither York nor Edinburgh was the last city visited, but one of them was the fourth.**

4. **Cardiff was visited immediately before Bath.**

5. **The visit to York did not immediately precede or follow a visit to London, but it did follow a trip to another city in England.**

Answer on page 185.

Interception

You've intercepted a message between a criminal who fled and his accomplice. But the message doesn't seem to make sense! Can you discover a piece of hidden information in the message?

TART HUH REAR ERE PEER
PEP BUMMER
THREAT PURR AREA SKIING NOUN
BITTER ROOT
BUSSING ARIA ANNO
BADDER DICING REED GORGE SOON

Answer on page 185.

Seen at the Scene (Part I)

Study this picture of the crime scene for 1 minute, then turn the page.

Seen at the Scene (Part II)

(Do not read this until you have read the previous page!)

1. What furniture did you see in the background?
  A. Bookshelf
  B. Rocking chair
  C. Sofa

2. The investigator is wearing protective booties over shoes.
  _____ True
  _____ False

3. The investigator is photographing this item.
  A. Briefcase / satchel
  B. An open book
  C. A woman's small purse

Answers on page 185.

Overheard Information (Part I)

Read the story below, then turn the page and answer the questions.

While on a train, a bystander overheard a woman tell a man about how best to rob a museum. The woman said, "They have two security guards monitoring the tapes, but one takes a half-hour break at 12:30 am and the other has been paid off. I'm going to leave a window open in the South side of the building, near the pottery exhibit. From there you just have to go through the guard's passageway to get to the gemstone exhibit. But remember, if you get caught and implicate me, I'm going to give evidence against you—and I have your fingerprints all over two artifacts from 2016."

Overheard Information (Part II)

(Do not read this until you have read the previous page!)

The bystander overheard the information about the crimes that were planned, but didn't have anywhere to write it down! Answer the questions below to help the bystander remember what to tell the police.

1. The thieves mention two exhibits.
>A. Masks and gems
>B. Pottery and gems
>C. Gems and artifacts
>D. Pottery and masks

2. One of the thieves was involved in an art theft in this year.
>A. 2006
>B. 2012
>C. 2016
>D. 2018

3. How many security guards will be on duty?
>A. At least two
>B. At least three
>C. Four
>D. Only one

4. The unlocked window will be found in this wing.
>A. South
>B. West
>C. East
>D. Basement

Answers on page 185.

Motel Hideout

A thief hides out in one of the 45 motel rooms listed in the chart below. The motel's in-house detective received a sheet of four clues, signed "The Logical Thief." Using these clues, the detective found the room number within 15 minutes—but by that time, the thief had fled. Can you find the thief's motel room more quickly?

1. **The number is either a multiple of 4 or has 4 as one of its digits, but not both.**
2. **The number is not divisible by 6, 7, or 8.**
3. **The first digit is larger than the second digit.**
4. **The number is not prime.**

51	52	53	54	55	56	57	58	59
41	42	43	44	45	46	47	48	49
31	32	33	34	35	36	37	38	39
21	22	23	24	25	26	27	28	29
11	12	13	14	15	16	17	18	19

Answer on page 185.

Alaska Davidson

Every word in all capitals below is contained within the group of letters. Words can be found in a straight line horizontally, vertically, or diagonally. They may be read either forward or backward.

The PACKARD family of OHIO left its STAMP on American HISTORY. Brothers JAMES Ward Packard and William DOUD Packard founded the AUTOMOBILE manufacturer NAMED after them. Sister ALASKA, later MARRIED to James DAVIDSON, was the FIRST female SPECIAL Agent in the PREDECESSOR of the FBI, the BUREAU of investigation.

In 1922, Alaska was 54 YEARS old when she BEGAN a new CAREER as a Special AGENT. She was HIRED by William BURNS, then DIRECTOR of the Bureau of INVESTIGATION. The Bureau wanted WOMEN to work on CASES related to the MANN Act against TRAFFICKING. Davidson WORKED in the WASHINGTON field OFFICE.

When J. Edgar HOOVER took over in 1924, he ASKED for Davidson's RESIGNATION. Two OTHER women also RESIGNED in the same TIME period, leaving the AGENCY without female agents for DECADES, until 1972.

```
H B S N A W A S H I N G T O N D X D
L O T Q G A D E K S A R L A P U Y E
N T A O E V P A E P E D G R W O E C
N J M F N L G S A V B E E Y T D W A
A G P F T E A C O O B D U R E R L D
M X O I N C K O Q X E Z A R X A X E
B U Y C H A H D L C F F B I S D R S
U T Y E R I E F E A F E M K O E N S
R T S D E R S S Z I X W A W T N O K
E E K R I L S T C A S O R O H G S R
A U M H I O I K O E Z M R R E I D O
U M P I R F I B M R E E I K R S I T
O H I O T N B A O U Y N E E H E V C
Y J V V G P J C K M R O D D K R A E
L V L A I C E P S V O D E M A N D R
X M I N V E S T I G A T I O N N V I
B O U W I L L I A M S B U R N S C D
C A R E E R A R E S I G N A T I O N
```

Murder in Colorado

Cryptograms are messages in substitution code. Break the code to read the message. For example, **THE SMART CAT** might become **FVO QWGDF JGF** if **F** is substituted for **T**, **V** for **H**, **O** for **E**, and so on.

OAS LSHRSM NOMQHXFSM EBFFSL PJ OI CBRS

TIGSH ZSOTSSH 1894 QHL 1903. OAS EBFFSM

GQV AQRS GPMLSMSL Q WFQBMRIVQHO TAI

AQL NPJJINSLFV XBRSH BHCIMGQOBIH OI

OAS QPOAIMBOBSN; NAS TQN CIPHL LSQL,

NOMQHXFSL. QFOAIPXA NSRSMQF GSH TSMS

NPNJSWON, OAS LSHRSM NOMQHXFSM TQN

HSRSM BLSHOBCBSL.

Answer on page 185.

The Fugitive's Itinerary

The letters in BOTSWANA can be found in boxes 2, 4, 5, 9, 17, 21, and 24, but not necessarily in that order. Similarly, the letters in all these words can be found in the boxes indicated. Your task is to insert all the letters of the alphabet into the boxes. If you do this correctly, the shaded cells will reveal what ties these words together.

Hint: Compare LIBYA and MALI to get the value of M, then MALI to CHAD to get the value of A.

Unused letter: X

BOTSWANA 2, 4, 5, 9, 17, 21, 24

BURKINA FASO 2, 3, 4, 6, 7, 9, 13, 17, 21, 25

CHAD 1, 10, 17, 18

CONGO 1, 2, 4, 15

DJIBOUTI 2, 3, 5, 7, 14, 18, 21

EGYPT 5, 8, 11, 15, 16

GAMBIA 7, 15, 17, 21, 23

IVORY COAST 1, 2, 5, 6, 7, 9, 11, 17, 19

KENYA 4, 8, 11, 13, 17

LIBYA 7, 11, 17, 21, 22

MALI 7, 17, 22, 23

MOZAMBIQUE 2, 3, 7, 8, 12, 17, 20, 21, 23

UGANDA 3, 4, 15, 17, 18

ZAMBIA 7, 12, 17, 21, 23

1	2	3	4	5	6	7	8	9	10	11	12	13

14	15	16	17	18	19	20	21	22	23	24	25	26
												X

Answers on page 185.

Track the Fugitive

The investigator is tracking the fugitive's past trips in order to find and recover information that was left behind in five cities. Each city was visited only once. Can you put together the travel timeline, using the information below?

1. **Rio de Janeiro was one of the final two cities visited.**

2. **The trip to Lima happened before the trip to Quito, but at least two other cities separated the visits.**

3. **From Santiago the fugitive went directly to either Quito or Rio.**

4. **The fugitive did not begin her travels in Buenos Aires.**

5. **The fugitive did not travel directly from Chile to Brazil.**

Answer on page 185.

Examine the two images below carefully. Are these sequences a match or not?

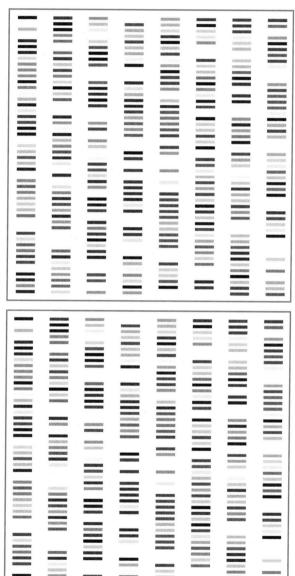

Motel Hideout

A thief hides out in one of the 45 motel rooms listed in the chart below. The motel's in-house detective received a sheet of four clues, signed "The Logical Thief." Using these clues, the detective found the room number within 15 minutes—but by that time, the thief had fled. Can you find the thief's motel room more quickly?

1. **The number is even.**
2. **The second digit is larger than the first.**
3. **The number is divisible by 4.**
4. **The number is not divisible by 6 or 7.**

51	52	53	54	55	56	57	58	59
41	42	43	44	45	46	47	48	49
31	32	33	34	35	36	37	38	39
21	22	23	24	25	26	27	28	29
11	12	13	14	15	16	17	18	19

Answer on page 185.

Overheard Information (Part I)

Read the story below, then turn the page and answer the questions.

While on a train, a bystander overheard a conversation between a man and a woman talking about how best to rob an antique store.

The woman says, "They lock up their money in the safe each night, and Jorie's given me the combo. 06-41-18. They go to the bank every Wednesday. They don't open until 10 AM and they never arrive themselves before 8, so let's go Wednesday before they open, about 6 AM."

The man says, "I've scoped out the video situation. They don't use their cameras to record—they just have them there to deter robberies. But the store on the left, the art gallery, has a camera on the front sidewalk—so we have to approach and leave from the back."

Overheard Information (Part II)

(Do not read this until you have read the previous page!)

The bystander overheard the information about the crimes that were planned, but didn't have anywhere to write it down! Answer the questions below to help the bystander remember what to tell the police.

1. Which statement about the overheard conversation is true?
   A. The conversation was between a man and a woman, and the woman spoke first.
   B. The conversation was between a man and a woman, and the man spoke first.
   C. The conversation was between two men.
   D. The conversation was between two women.

2. The combo for the safe is:
   A. 66-41-18
   B. 60-41-18
   C. 06-41-18
   D. 06-14-18

3. The theft is planned for this day and time.
   A. Tuesday about 6 PM
   B. Wednesday around 6 AM
   C. Wednesday around 8 AM
   D. Wednesday around 10 AM

4. The name of the accomplice who gave the safe code is:
   A. Jorie
   B. Joey
   C. Jordy
   D. Jolie

Answers on page 186.

Good at Getting Free

Cryptograms are messages in substitution code. Break the code to read the message. For example, **THE SMART CAT** might become **FVO QWGDF JGF** if **F** is substituted for **T**, **V** for **H**, **O** for **E**, and so on.

AOIHNINI HSQPH HSBBSJ KSXBDI NJTSENH

FIDA EIPJDC CD FNVNI KYSC FDOI KPANJ. YN

VSJ SHHNH KD KYN ADJK VSCKNH BPJK PC

1953 SCH VSJ TSOLYK S FNV ADCKYJ BSKNI.

Answer on page 186.

Catch the Suspect

Can you catch the suspect before she finishes getting through the maze?

START

FINISH

Answer on page 186.

Ways to Get Away

Unscramble each word or phrase below to reveal a word or phrase related to fleeing an investigation.

ON OR FUTON (3 words)

AVIARY DEW (2 words)

DRAIN RITE (2 words)

A PRALINE (1 word)

ADIEU GUSSIES (3 words)

SAUNA AISLE (3 words)

BEGAN OUST (4 words)

BELCHED WIND TORN (4 words)

Answers on page 186.

Track the Fugitive

The investigator is tracking the fugitive's past trips in order to find and recover information that was left behind in five cities. Each city was visited only once. Can you put together the travel timeline, using the information below?

1. **The fugitive did not travel from Austin to Dallas or vice versa.**

2. **The fugitive traveled to Portland from Nashville, with a stop at one other city in between.**

3. **The fugitive traveled from one city that starts with D immediately to the next, in alphabetical order.**

4. **Austin was not the last city visited.**

5. **Denver was one of the first three cities visited.**

Answer on page 186.

Motel Hideout

A thief hides out in one of the 45 motel rooms listed in the chart below. The motel's in-house detective received a sheet of four clues, signed "The Logical Thief." Using these clues, the detective found the room number within 15 minutes—but by that time, the thief had fled. Can you find the thief's motel room more quickly?

1. **3 is one of the digits.**
2. **The number is not prime.**
3. **The sum of the digits is larger than 5.**
4. **The number is divisible by 4.**

51	52	53	54	55	56	57	58	59
41	42	43	44	45	46	47	48	49
31	32	33	34	35	36	37	38	39
21	22	23	24	25	26	27	28	29
11	12	13	14	15	16	17	18	19

DNA Sequence

Examine the two images below carefully. Are these sequences a match or not?

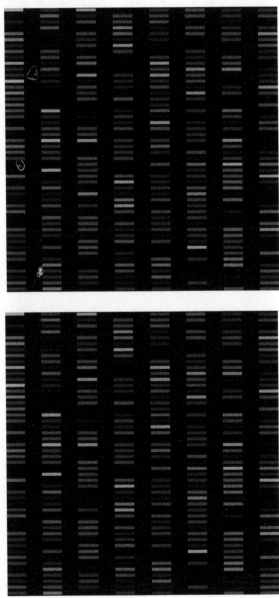

Answer on page 186.

Making a List, Checking It Twice

Cryptograms are messages in substitution code. Break the code to read the message. For example, **THE SMART CAT** might become **FVO QWGDF JGF** if **F** is substituted for **T**, **V** for **H**, **O** for **E**, and so on.

BZIK XRCFXR ACBNCM RBQRQ OD CB NYR

ACMN TGBNRQ LZMN BCN CBIR HON NTZIR.

ACBNCM TGM G ARAHRF CS NYR IYZIGXC

CONSZN. YR TGM DLGIRQ CB NYR LZMN

SCLLCTZBX CBR FCHHRFV, GBQ NYRB GQQRQ

GXGZB GSNRF G DFZMCB RMIGDR.

Public Enemy #1: John Dillinger

Every word in all capitals below is contained within the group of letters. Words can be found in a straight line horizontally, vertically, or diagonally. They may be read either forward or backward.

John **DILLINGER** was **ONLY** 31 years **OLD** when he **DIED**, but his **LEGEND** lived on in **MEDIA** and **HISTORY**. **JOHN** Dillinger was **ACTIVE** during the **GREAT DEPRESSION**. He was **SEEN** as **LARGER** than **LIFE** for his daring **ESCAPES** from prison and his **BRAVADO** while **ROBBING** banks.

He **MAY** at one **POINT** have escaped from **PRISON** with a **FAKE** gun, or a real **GUN** that he never shot. He **REPORTEDLY** had **PLASTIC** surgery to **CHANGE** his **APPEARANCE** and used **ACID** to **OBLITERATE** his **FINGERPRINTS**.

Dillinger was **SHOT** by **FEDERAL** agents outside the **BIOGRAPH** Theater, having just seen a **CRIME** drama called "**MANHATTAN** Melodrama."

```
J F A K E K M E V I T C A D Y N
E W F R E P O R T E D L Y D O L
M S A L H C H A N G E D L I S I
I T H A I E P J O H N O S H D F
R N P R S X T D M E S S O P E E
C I A E T F B A G O E T R W I M
M R R D O O C E R R D E N R D A
M P G E R S L I P E G A R I P X
A R O F Y N E E P N T O V P O C
N E I E O D P I R B I E A I P
H G B E N T L L A B I A L T R M
A N S L A A L Q I C R S S B E B
T I Y E R I D N Z A S A O D O B
T F R G D G G I N E L E I N G Y
A G E T U U C C C P Z A T T D O
N R O N I L E W O A S G E M A Y
```

Find and Catch

Change just one letter on each line to go from the top word to the bottom word. Do not change the order of the letters. You must have a common English word at each step.

FINDS

_____

_____

_____ **to burn just a little bit**

_____

_____

_____

_____

_____

CATCH

Answers on page 187.

Track the Fugitive

The investigator is tracking the fugitive's past trips in order to find and recover information that was left behind in five cities. Each city was visited only once. Can you put together the travel timeline, using the information below?

1. **Brussels and Moscow were separated by exactly two other cities. Either Brussels or Moscow could have been the earlier visit.**

2. **Ankara was not the third place visited.**

3. **Tunis and Athens were visited back to back, but not necessarily in that order.**

4. **The visit to Athens preceded the trip to Ankara, but not immediately.**

5. **One of the cities that starts with A was followed immediately by a trip to the city that starts with B.**

Answer on page 187.

Flee by Foot

The letters in BOOT can be found in boxes 3, 12, and 22 but not necessarily in that order. Similarly, the letters in all the other types of shoes can be found in the boxes indicated. Your task is to insert all the letters of the alphabet into the boxes. If you do this correctly, the shaded cells will reveal the name of another type of shoe.

Hint: Compare MULE and PUMP to get the value of P, then PUMP and MOCCASIN for the values of M and U. Unused letters: J, Q

BOOT: 3, 12, 22

BROGUE: 3, 4, 10, 12, 16, 18

CHOPINE: 1, 3, 7, 9, 11, 15, 16

GYM SHOE: 3, 4, 5, 15, 16, 17, 24

LOAFER: 2, 3, 6, 10, 13, 16

MOCCASIN: 1, 3, 5, 6, 7, 9, 17

MULE: 2, 16, 17, 18

OVERSHOE: 3, 5, 10, 15, 16, 19

OXFORD: 3, 8, 10, 13, 23

PUMP: 11, 17, 18

SANDAL: 2, 5, 6, 9, 23

SLIPPER: 2, 5, 7, 10, 11, 16

SNEAKER: 5, 6, 9, 10, 14, 16

WEDGE: 4, 16, 21, 23

ZORI: 3, 7, 10, 20

1	2	3	4	5	6	7	8	9	10	11	12	13

14	15	16	17	18	19	20	21	22	23	24	25	26
											J	Q

Answers on page 187.

Overheard Information (Part I)

Read the story below, then turn the page and answer the questions.

An investigator hears a conversation where a jewel thief boasts to a friend about her "accomplishments." She says, "You'd be amazed at how many people don't even keep track of their belongings! I went to the Wright party in June 2018, you wouldn't have even recognized me, it was when I had the Trish Bailey ID. I picked up the nicest diamond ring and a set of opal earrings, and they didn't even spot the theft and report it until eleven months later. Imagine having so much jewelry you don't even notice when some goes missing for the better part of a year!"

Overheard Information (Part II)

(Do not read this until you have read the previous page!)

1. The theft described took place at this party.

    A. Wright

    B. Bailey

    C. Baley

    D. The name is not given.

2. The thief used this alias at the party.

    A. Trish

    B. Patrice

    C. Tricia

    D. Patsy

3. The following items were stolen.

    A. A diamond ring and a set of opal earrings

    B. Diamond earrings and an opal ring

    C. Diamond earrings and an opal necklace

    D. A diamond ring and an opal necklace

4. When was the theft reported?

    A. Immediately

    B. Six months later

    C. Nine months later

    D. Eleven months later

Answers on page 187.

Murder in New Orleans

Cryptograms are messages in substitution code. Break the code to read the message. For example, **THE SMART CAT** might become **FVO QWGDF JGF** if **F** is substituted for **T**, **V** for **H**, **O** for **E**, and so on.

AH 1918 FHT 1919, F GFH VAQB FH FWY

QYOOIOAZYT HYV IOEYFHP VAQB BAP

GROTYOP AH QBY AQFEAFH-FGYOAUFH

UIGGRHAQX. BAP GROTYO PKOYY PQIKKYT

FNORKQEX, EYFSAHM QBY UFPY RHPIESYT

JIOYSYO.

Mystery Writers

ACROSS

1. Peach or plum, e.g.
6. Supermodel Campbell
11. Inflexible
12. One who puts you in your place?
13. "The Pelican Brief" author
15. Genteel socials
16. Bk. before Jeremiah
17. Mountain ___ (soft drinks)
20. Soup tin
22. Biological eggs
23. Curving inward
27. His mysteries and thrillers have many a twist
29. Actress Bening or Funicello
30. English "Inc."
31. Edison's monogram
32. Psychiatrist's appt.
33. MPG rating agency
36. Conversational gap
38. TV's "Bones" was based on her forensic thrillers
43. Spiritual mentors
44. Goodbye, in Acapulco
45. What italicized letters do
46. Give a noncommittal answer

DOWN

1. Basketball's Erving, familiarly
2. Copacabana Beach setting
3. "Gross!"
4. Half-___ (pipsqueaks)
5. Barely beat, with "out"
6. Annoyance
7. Biblical jawbone source
8. "I wasn't expecting you!"
9. Ft. or in.
10. Cookbook author Rombauer
14. Storyteller
17. Qatar's capital
18. Novelist ___ Hunter
19. Give a heads-up to
21. Army cpl. or sgt.
23. It makes things happen
24. Having what it takes
25. Ex-servicemen
26. Reaches a conclusion
28. Serve that's replayed
32. Playground ride
33. Cardiology tests, briefly
34. Actor Newman or Muni
35. Gillette razor
37. "The King of Queens" actress Remini
39. Mongol invader
40. "El ___" (Spanish hero)
41. Take all of, as the covers
42. 180 degrees from NNW

Interception

You've intercepted a message between a criminal who fled and his accomplice. It might be the criminal's current location, but there are four place names listed. Can you discover the criminal's current location hidden in the message?

ALGIERS
SEOUL
FORT WORTH
IDAHO

Answer on page 187.

Study this picture of the crime scene for 1 minute, then turn the page.

Seen at the Scene (Part II)

(Do not read this until you have read the previous page!)

1. The investigator is near this item of furniture.

    A. Kitchen table

    B. Desk

    C. End table

2. What item is seen in the picture?

    A. Ceramic mug of coffee

    B. Paper cup with lid

    C. Plastic water bottle

3. The investigator is wearing gloves.

    _____ True

    _____ False

Answers on page 187.

Motel Hideout

A thief hides out in one of the 45 motel rooms listed in the chart below. The motel's in-house detective received a sheet of four clues, signed "The Logical Thief." Using these clues, the detective found the room number within 15 minutes—but by that time, the thief had fled. Can you find the thief's motel room more quickly?

1. **The number is divisible by 3.**
2. **The first digit and the second digit are not consecutive numbers (for example, neither 12 nor 54).**
3. **The number is not divisible by 11, 13, 15, 17, or 19.**
4. **If you multiply the digits together, the result is neither a multiple of 8 nor contains the digit 8.**

51	52	53	54	55	56	57	58	59
41	42	43	44	45	46	47	48	49
31	32	33	34	35	36	37	38	39
21	22	23	24	25	26	27	28	29
11	12	13	14	15	16	17	18	19

Answer on page 187.

Mark Felt

Every word in all capitals below is contained within the group of letters. Words can be found in a straight line horizontally, vertically, or diagonally. They may be read either forward or backward.

G-Man **WILLIAM** Mark **FELT** was an **ASSOCIATE** Director at the FBI who **CHANGED** American **HISTORY** when he **ACTED** as the **ANONYMOUS** source **"DEEP THROAT"** who **INFORMED** "The **WASHINGTON** Post" reporters Woodward and **BERNSTEIN** about **DETAILS** of the **WATERGATE** scandal. Their **REPORTS** rocked the country.

Felt **BEGAN** work for the **FEDERAL** Bureau of **INVESTIGATION** in 1942 and **WORKED** there for several **DECADES**. Though Felt published a **MEMOIR** in 1979, he did not **MENTION** his role as Deep Throat. While there were **RUMORS** that he was Woodward's **INFORMANT**, that was not **CONFIRMED** until 2005.

```
S  X  N  C  O  N  F  I  R  M  E  D  I  S  I  A
U  S  B  O  Z  E  S  W  G  S  G  Z  E  C  I  V
O  B  L  B  I  I  T  E  M  D  M  T  S  A  N  C
M  R  E  I  H  T  Q  A  G  E  A  I  U  C  F  C
Y  A  I  R  A  V  A  Y  I  G  N  Y  E  T  O  H
N  L  I  O  N  T  T  G  R  C  X  T  F  E  R  A
O  A  K  B  M  S  E  E  I  D  O  Z  I  D  M  N
N  R  D  L  F  E  T  D  E  T  D  S  V  O  A  G
A  E  E  D  U  A  M  E  W  S  S  B  S  B  N  E
A  D  K  C  W  U  P  I  I  L  E  E  E  A  T  D
T  E  R  C  U  T  L  V  A  N  Q  D  V  G  L  Y
L  F  O  B  H  L  S  R  O  M  U  R  A  N  A  C
E  L  W  R  I  M  R  E  P  O  R  T  S  C  I  N
F  P  O  A  C  H  I  S  T  O  R  Y  L  N  E  I
M  A  M  T  D  N  O  T  G  N  I  H  S  A  W  D
T  U  B  K  P  F  E  D  E  M  R  O  F  N  I  G
```

Track the Fugitive

The investigator is tracking the fugitive's past trips in order to find and recover information that was left behind in five cities. Each city was visited only once. Can you put together the travel timeline, using the information below?

1. **Skopje was visited sometime before Stockholm.**
2. **Riyadh was visited sometime after Seoul, but not immediately after.**
3. **Dodoma was one of the first three cities visited.**
4. **None of the cities that start with S were visited back to back.**

Answer on page 187.

Examine the two images below carefully. Are these sequences a match or not?

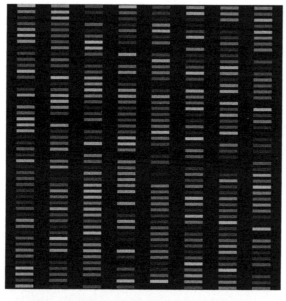

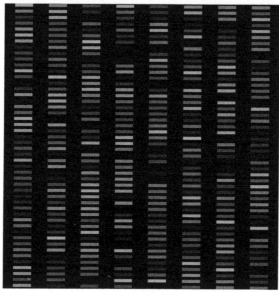

Answer on page 188.

Murder at the Party

The letters in BANQUET can be found in boxes 5, 7, 10, 15, 19, 21, and 22 but not necessarily in that order. Similarly, the letters in all the other party things can be found in the boxes indicated. Your task is to insert all the letters of the alphabet into the boxes. If you do this correctly, the shaded cells will reveal the name of other party things.

Hint: Compare HOSTESS and TOASTS to get the values of A, then FAVORS and FLOWERS for the values of V. Unused letters: J, X

BANQUET: 5, 7, 10, 15, 19, 21, 22

BUFFET: 7, 10, 12, 15, 22

CENTERPIECE: 1, 3, ,7, 9, 15, 18, 21

DANCE BAND: 1, 5, 7, 10, 11, 21

DOOR PRIZE: 2, 3, 7, 8, 9, 11, 18

FAVORS: 2, 3, 4, 5, 12, 23

FLOWERS: 2, 3, 4, 7, 12, 17, 20

GUESTS: 4, 6, 7, 15, 22

HORS D'OEUVRES: 2, 3, 4, 7, 11, 13, 22, 23

HOSTESS: 2, 4, 7, 13, 15

MUSIC: 1, 4, 9, 22, 24

NOISEMAKERS: 2, 3, 4, 5, 7, 9, 14, 21, 24

PARTY HATS: 3, 4, 5, 13, 15, 16, 18

PUNCH: 1, 13, 18, 21, 22

TOASTS: 2, 4, 5, 15

1	2	3	4	5	6	7	8	9	10	11	12	13

14	15	16	17	18	19	20	21	22	23	24	25	26
											J	X

Answers on page 188.

Overheard Information (Part I)

Read the story below, then turn the page and answer the questions.

An investigator hears a conversation between two criminals, in which one tells the other the passwords to the underground gambling clubs run through his chain of restaurants. He hears, "At the Oakmont location, ask for Leo and tell him, 'Didn't you used to have lemon bars for dessert?' At Golden Circle Plaza, ask for Roger and tell him, 'Say, do you have a cousin named Rhoda?' But Roger's only there Tuesday, Thursday, and Sunday. Don't go to the place on Truman until things cool down, since the cops are watching that location."

Overheard Information (Part II)

(Do not read this until you have read the previous page!)

1. Who is in charge at the Oakmont location?

_____

2. Where does Roger work?

_____

3. On what days does Roger work?

_____

4. What is the password at the Oakmont location?

_____

Answers on page 188.

A local bank was robbed! The bank has a poster up in its lobby, detailing what they know about the robbers. Read the page, then turn the page to answer questions.

Date: November 18, 2020

Time: 4:56 PM

Suspect descriptions:

Suspect #1: 5'8", short brown hair, wearing a mask of George Clooney. Tellers said that the voice seemed female.

Suspect #2: 5'5", short blond hair (dyed with dark roots), wearing a mask of Brad Pitt. Tellers said that the voice could be male or female.

Weapons: Machine guns

Getaway vehicle: motorcycles. Washington state license plates, partial plate N87

Bank Robbery Alert (Part II)

(Do not read this until you have read the previous page!)

Fill in all the information you remember.

Date: _____

Time: _____

Suspect descriptions:

Suspect 1: _____

_____

Suspect 2:

_____

_____

Weapons: _____

Getaway vehicle: _____

Answers on page 188.

A Long Escape

Cryptograms are messages in substitution code. Break the code to read the message. For example, **THE SMART CAT** might become **FVO QWGDF JGF** if **F** is substituted for **T**, **V** for **H**, **O** for **E**, and so on.

XLKDA XLYMUSKOYLM SKM MYDOYDIYH OE

FLPMED KXOYL UY KIIPHYDOKBBV APBBYH

K CKD SUPBY MFYYHPDW. KXOYL MYLRPDW

MECY OPCY, UY SKM KO KD "UEDEL XKLC"

XKIPBPOV, SUPIU UY OUYD YMIKFYH PD 1959.

UY SKM OLKIAYH HESD EDIY PD 1975 PD

SYMO RPLWPDPK, JQO SKM LYBYKMYH

KXOYL UPM IECCQDPOV KDH OUY MOKOY'M

WERYLDEL REQIUYH XEL UPC KDH

HPMKFFYKLYH KWKPD. UY SKM XEQDH KDH

KLLYMOYH PD 2015 JQO LYBYKMYH 2016.

Answer on page 188.

Find the Fugitive

Can you track the fugitive to the center of the labyrinth?

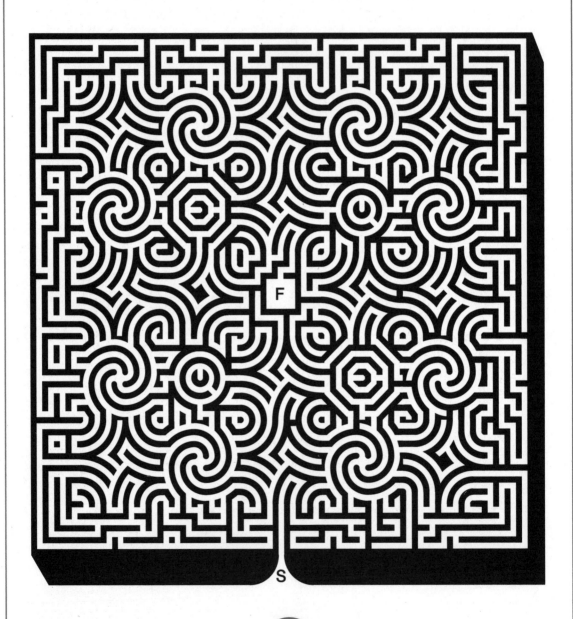

Answer on page 188.

Motel Hideout

A thief hides out in one of the 45 motel rooms listed in the chart below. The motel's in-house detective received a sheet of four clues, signed "The Logical Thief." Using these clues, the detective found the room number within 15 minutes—but by that time, the thief had fled. Can you find the thief's motel room more quickly?

1. **The number is prime.**
2. **The second digit is larger than the first.**
3. **If you multiply the digits, the resulting number is prime.**
4. **The sum of the digits is less than 7.**

51	52	53	54	55	56	57	58	59
41	42	43	44	45	46	47	48	49
31	32	33	34	35	36	37	38	39
21	22	23	24	25	26	27	28	29
11	12	13	14	15	16	17	18	19

Answer on page 188.

Track the Fugitive

The investigator is tracking the fugitive's past trips in order to find and recover information that was left behind in five cities. Each city was visited only once. Can you put together the travel timeline, using the information below?

1. **From San Diego the fugitive went directly to the other city in California.**

2. **The fugitive went from Butte, Montana, to Des Moines, Iowa, but not directly. There was a stop in between.**

3. **Cleveland, Ohio, was one of the first two cities visited.**

4. **Sacramento was one of the final two cities visited.**

5. **When the fugitive arrived in Cleveland, it was from the West.**

Answer on page 188.

Murder in Georgia

Cryptograms are messages in substitution code. Break the code to read the message. For example, **THE SMART CAT** might become **FVO QWGDF JGF** if **F** is substituted for **T**, **V** for **H**, **O** for **E**, and so on.

ZP ENZOP HAHPNNG ZPEZGPZ TJFNG

TNMN FQMRNMNR WNPTNNG 1909 ZGR

1914 WX Z KNMOJG RQWWNR PBN

"ZPEZGPZ MAKKNM." PBN DAEENM

HJUQONR JG XJQGI WEZUD TJFNG AG

PBNAM 20O. BN TZO GNSNM UZQIBP.

Every word in all capitals below is contained within the group of letters. Words can be found in a straight line horizontally, vertically, or diagonally. They may be read either forward or backward.

He was born **LESTER** Joseph **GILLIS** in 1908, but he was **KNOWN** as **GEORGE** Nelson or **BABY** Face **NELSON**. The bank **ROBBER** and partner-in-crime with **JOHN** Dillinger **NEVER** had a **CHANCE** to grow out of the **MONIKER**, as he was **ONLY** 25 when he **DIED**.

He was first **ARRESTED** at the age of 12 for accidentally **SHOOTING** another **CHILD**, and was sent to the state **REFORMATORY** for a **YEAR**. Other early crimes included car **THEFT**, **JOYRIDING**, stripping cars of **TIRES**, and shipping **BOOTLEG** alcohol. He moved on to **ARMED** robbery, both of **BANKS** and private **CITIZENS**. In the **COURSE** of robbing places like **TAVERNS** and **ROADHOUSES**, he **ENGAGED** in **MURDER**.

After a **SHOOTOUT** with federal **AGENTS** in **WISCONSIN** in April 1934, during which Nelson killed an agent, Nelson was **DECLARED** Public **ENEMY** #1. Nelson moved around the **COUNTRY** to avoid the **MANHUNT**, but was **TRACKED** down in **NOVEMBER** 1934 and died in a shootout in **BARRINGTON**, Illinois.

```
Q  I  D  B  O  O  T  L  E  G  S  P  Y  S  K  R  N  Q
R  L  E  A  R  R  E  S  T  E  D  N  E  B  E  W  Y  C
E  S  R  U  O  C  E  Y  L  N  O  R  R  T  N  M  M  H
L  H  A  N  T  A  N  N  F  S  I  J  S  E  O  G  E  A
A  J  L  B  E  H  R  G  G  T  G  E  T  A  V  E  N  N
C  O  C  W  O  L  D  M  N  A  L  I  H  G  E  A  E  C
N  Y  E  J  I  J  S  R  E  I  G  R  V  E  M  L  T  E
Y  R  D  J  B  S  O  O  T  D  T  E  R  N  B  K  D  N
R  I  E  F  B  B  C  H  N  B  C  O  D  T  E  N  I  M
T  D  B  V  B  D  E  O  T  M  A  I  O  S  R  O  E  O
N  I  J  E  E  F  L  A  N  D  U  S  T  H  N  W  D  N
U  N  R  D  T  N  U  I  H  S  K  R  I  I  S  N  E  I
O  G  T  U  O  T  O  O  H  S  I  X  D  L  Z  U  Z  K
C  Z  Y  E  A  R  U  Z  L  C  C  N  E  E  L  E  F  E
N  Y  B  A  B  S  G  E  O  R  G  E  J  V  R  I  N  R
N  S  Q  F  E  Y  R  O  T  A  M  R  O  F  E  R  G  S
Y  Z  N  S  Z  B  A  N  K  S  K  T  R  A  C  K  E  D
B  A  R  R  I  N  G  T  O  N  M  A  N  H  U  N  T  C
```

Describe the Criminal's Hairdo

The letters in BANGS can be found in boxes 3, 6, 14, 18, and 20 but not necessarily in that order. Similarly, the letters in all the other hairdos can be found in the boxes indicated. Your task is to insert all the letters of the alphabet into the boxes. If you do this correctly, the shaded cells will reveal the name of another hairdo.

Hint: Compare PONYTAIL and PIGTAIL to get the value of G, then BUN and BANGS for the value of U. Unused letters, J, Q, and X

BANGS: 3, 6, 14, 18, 20

BEEHIVE: 4, 8, 14, 17, 19

BOUFFANT: 3, 5, 10, 12, 14, 15, 18

BRAIDS: 3, 4, 6, 9, 14, 21

BUN: 10, 14, 18

CHIGNON: 4, 12, 16, 17, 18, 20

CURLS: 2, 6, 9, 10, 16

FRIZZ: 4, 9, 11, 15

MARCEL WAVE: 2, 3, 8, 9, 13, 16, 19, 22

PAGEBOY: 1, 3, 8, 12, 14, 20, 23

PERMANENT: 1, 3, 5, 8, 9, 13, 18

PIGTAIL: 1, 2, 3, 4, 5, 20

PONYTAIL: 1, 2, 3, 4, 5, 12, 18, 23

RINGLETS: 2, 4, 5, 6, 8, 9, 18, 20

TOPKNOT: 1, 5, 7, 12, 18

1	2	3	4	5	6	7	8	9	10	11	12	13
14	15	16	17	18	19	20	21	22	23	24	25	26
										J	Q	X

Answers on page 189.

Examine the two images below carefully. Are these sequences a match or not?

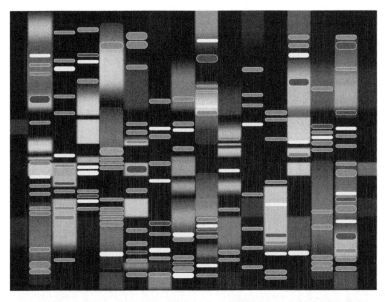

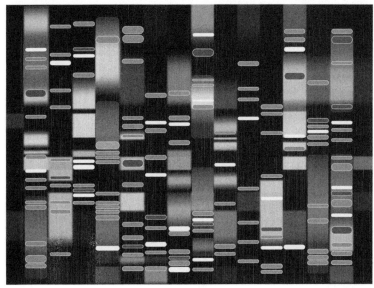

Answer on page 189.

Fond of Robbing Banks

Cryptograms are messages in substitution code. Break the code to read the message. For example, **THE SMART CAT** might become **FVO QWGDF JGF** if **F** is substituted for **T**, **V** for **H**, **O** for **E**, and so on.

C GCFB LHGGRL HM PYR 1940O CFJ

1950O, MLRJRLZNB WLCFP JQFF

TCO NCDDRJ "PYR EHJRLF AHYF

JZDDZFWRL." CMPRL CF RONCIR MLHE

NQOPHJV ZF 1958, YR TCO CJJRJ PH

PYR EHOP TCFPRJ DZOP. YR TCO MHQFJ

JRCJ MLHE NCQORO QFBFHTF ZF 1959.

138

Answer on page 189.

Overheard Information (Part I)

Read the story below, then turn the page and answer the questions.

A bystander heard two people talking at a coffee shop, only to realize they were counterfeiters! One said to the other, "The order is forty-two $20 dollar bills, fifty $50 bills, and seventy-seven $10 bills. I've left it all in the safe, and the temporary combination is 57-89-10. You need to pick it up by Wednesday at 4 PM or the money is removed."

Overheard Information (Part II)

(Do not read this until you have read the previous page!)

1. How many bills of each denomination are being delivered? (For some, the answer may be zero.)

$5: _____

$10: _____

$20: _____

$50: _____

$100: _____

2. What is the combination for the safe?

_____

3. What is the deadline to pick up the delivery?

_____

Answers on page 189.

Motel Hideout

A thief hides out in one of the 45 motel rooms listed in the chart below. The motel's in-house detective received a sheet of four clues, signed "The Logical Thief." Using these clues, the detective found the room number within 15 minutes—but by that time, the thief had fled. Can you find the thief's motel room more quickly?

1. **The sum of the digits is less than 10.**

2. **When you multiple the digits together, the resulting number is less than 10.**

3. **The number is prime.**

4. **If you reverse the order of the digits, the resulting number is not found on the chart.**

51	52	53	54	55	56	57	58	59
41	42	43	44	45	46	47	48	49
31	32	33	34	35	36	37	38	39
21	22	23	24	25	26	27	28	29
11	12	13	14	15	16	17	18	19

Answer on page 189.

Track the Fugitive

The investigator is tracking the fugitive's past trips in order to find and recover information that was left behind in five cities. Each city was visited only once. Can you put together the travel timeline, using the information below?

1. **Panama City was neither the first nor the final city on the list.**
2. **Caracas was either the first or third city.**
3. **Quito was visited sometime after La Paz.**
4. **Montevideo is one of the final two cities.**
5. **From Venezuela, the fugitive went immediately to Ecuador's capital city.**

Answer on page 189.

A Successful Disappearance

Cryptograms are messages in substitution code. Break the code to read the message. For example, **THE SMART CAT** might become **FVO QWGDF JGF** if **F** is substituted for **T**, **V** for **H**, **O** for **E**, and so on.

ZEZTGIM ATMFTG, CIMG BG BIUT,

RBOTKKZTMZR TP PJZ TNZ IH 39. BG 1933,

ATMFTG, JZM CIWHMBZGR, TGR TGIPJZM

FTG PMBZR PI MIC T YEIPJBGN OPIMZ.

ATMFTG'O TYYIFKEBYZ OJIP PJZ OPIMZ

IUGZM. ATMFTG OZMSZR OZSZG WZTMO

BG KMBOIG CZHIMZ OJZ ZOYTKZR PI

OZZ JZM HTFBEW. HMIF PJZMZ OJZ

RBOTKKZTMZR, YIFFQGBYTPBGN UBPJ

JZM HTFBEW SBT GZUOKTKZM TRO.

Robert B. Parker Books

ACROSS

1. Apt anagram of "notes"
6. Be a braggart
11. Folded Mexican snacks
12. Award named for Poe
13. Spenser and Hawk battle a street gang in the 19th Spenser novel
15. Balcony section
16. Barely squeeze by (with "out")
17. Suffer from overexercise, maybe
20. In literature, Pussycat's friend
22. Life force, in Taoism
23. Like the Cheshire Cat
27. Eighth novel about Parker's Massachusetts cop Jesse Stone
29. Bouncing off the walls
30. Back talk
31. "The Whiffenpoof Song" singer
32. Hair styling substances
33. Charged particle
36. Narrow wood strip
38. Parker's sixth book about his private eye Sunny Randall
43. Gold fabrics
44. Boris, to Bullwinkle
45. Vote in
46. Dull photo finish

DOWN

1. Norm, for short
2. "The Way" of Lao Tzu
3. Bygone French coin
4. Barnes's business partner
5. Home to the Kon-Tiki Museum
6. Moistening
7. Admiring poem
8. Dickensian chill
9. Drop the quarterback
10. Yuletide buy
14. More than a swellhead
17. Adolescent woe
18. Fashionable and stylish
19. Like a soprano's voice
21. Lawyer's deg.
23. Most quiet
24. Like a loafer
25. Get just right
26. Hoodwinks
28. Clod buster
32. Accra's nation
33. It is surrounded by water
34. Gem for a Scorpio, perhaps
35. Rumpelstiltskin's secret
37. Opponent of "us"
39. Red VCR button
40. Fish tank accessory
41. Basic time standard: Abbr.
42. CBS symbol

Escape or Not?

Can you escape by rappelling over the side of the building?

Answer on page 190.

Flees the Scene

Change just one letter on each line to go from the top word to the bottom word. Do not change the order of the letters. You must have a common English word at each step.

FLEES

‾‾‾‾‾‾

‾‾‾‾‾‾

‾‾‾‾‾‾

‾‾‾‾‾‾‾   **Water vehicles**

‾‾‾‾‾‾

‾‾‾‾‾‾

‾‾‾‾‾‾

‾‾‾‾‾‾

‾‾‾‾‾‾

‾‾‾‾‾‾

SCENE

Answers on page 190.

Interception

You've intercepted a message between a criminal who fled and his accomplice. From other information, you know this is supposed to contain the location of a key to a safe deposit box. But the message doesn't seem to make sense! Can you discover where the key is found?

**IRON SARI DECIDE
OVER AGAIN GLUE
VIA SIDE**

Answer on page 190.

The Fugitive's Alias

The letters in BARBARA can be found in boxes 2, 3, and 20 but not necessarily in that order. Similarly, the letters in all the other women's names can be found in the boxes indicated. Your task is to insert all the letters of the alphabet into the boxes. If you do this correctly, the shaded cells will reveal another female name.

BARBARA: 2, 3, 20

DENISE: 6, 7, 8, 12, 21

ELIZABETH: 2, 5, 6, 8, 11, 13, 20, 25

FAYE: 2, 8, 14, 26

GRACE: 1, 2, 3, 8, 19

JOYCE: 1, 4, 8, 14, 17

JULIET: 5, 6, 8, 9, 13, 17

KAREN: 2, 3, 7, 8, 18

MARY: 2, 3, 14, 23

PHYLLIS: 5, 6, 12, 14, 24, 25

RAQUEL: 2, 3, 5, 8, 9, 16

ROXANNE: 2, 3, 4, 7, 8, 10

VIVIAN: 2, 6, 7, 22

WANDA: 2, 7, 15, 21

1	2	3	4	5	6	7	8	9	10	11	12	13

14	15	16	17	18	19	20	21	22	23	24	25	26

Every word in all capitals below is contained within the group of letters. Words can be found in a straight line horizontally, vertically, or diagonally. They may be read either forward or backward.

CHARLES Arthur FLOYD was BORN in 1904 and became a BANK robber during the DEPRESSION. As he ROBBED the banks, he reportedly BURNED documents related to MORTGAGES, so he BECAME a bit of a FOLK HERO to people in DEBT. This may, HOWEVER, be a folk TALE.

In 1933, Floyd was a SUSPECT in a GUNFIGHT between criminals and law ENFORCEMENT officers where FOUR died. Floyd DENIED involvement.

In 1934, Floyd was KILLED. Account DIVERGE as to whether it was LOCAL law enforcement or the FBI. Before he DIED, he denied INVOLVEMENT in the Kansas City MASSACRE one more TIME. More than 20,000 PEOPLE flocked to his FUNERAL in OKLAHOMA.

```
B I O U O Q T R L I G M R Y M Z Y
O T C A E A N D A D E B T O O T E
R T N O I S S E R P E D R B A M U
N T N E A Z L Q M L T T K L A D D
I N E E L C S O B Q G T E C R E F
I E D R M P H G C A J L E O O N L
R M Z G C E O A G A K B L K B R O
V E D K I A C E R W L J A L B U Y
A V V E N U S R P L X I R A E B D
E L F E N A T S O O E G E H D G F
G O O O W I B D A F G S N O D I B
R V Z K L O E V T M N N U M E R I
E N Z E V K H D M B X E F A C J B
V I J E D X H D J T H G I F N U G
I B R S U S P E C T A D E L L I K
D U T L O H R R R T D E I D G T G
H C S Y E M I T M O S G O F O U R
```

Track the Fugitive

The investigator is tracking the fugitive's past trips in order to find and recover information that was left behind in five cities. Each city was visited only once. Can you put together the travel timeline, using the information below?

1. **Madrid and Warsaw were visited back to back, not necessarily in that order.**

2. **Riga was visited before Zagreb, with exactly one other stop in between.**

3. **Oslo was either the second or third stop.**

4. **Warsaw was not the final stop.**

Answer on page 190.

Seen at the Scene (Part I)

Study this picture of the crime scene for 1 minute, then turn the page.

Seen at the Scene (Part II)

(Do not read this until you have read the previous page!)

1. How many evidence markers do you see in the picture?

    A. 3, numbered 1 through 3

    B. 4, numbered 1 through 4

    C. 4, numbered 1, 3, 4, 5

2. The gun is found at this evidence marker.

    A. 1

    B. 2

    C. 3

3. The arm seen in the photo is wearing a wristwatch.

    _____ True

    _____ False

Answers on page 190.

Examine the two images below carefully. Are these sequences a match or not?

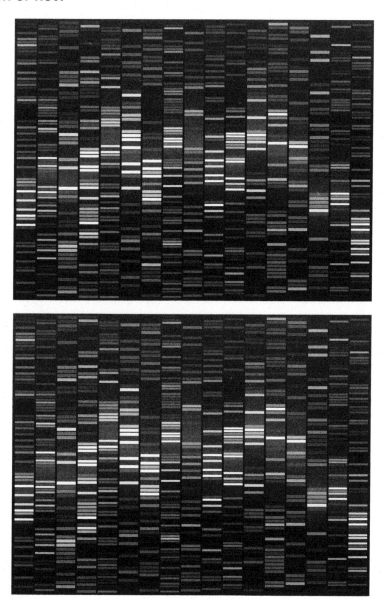

Answer on page 190.

Motel Hideout

A thief hides out in one of the 45 motel rooms listed in the chart below. The motel's in-house detective received a sheet of four clues, signed "The Logical Thief." Using these clues, the detective found the room number within 15 minutes—but by that time, the thief had fled. Can you find the thief's motel room more quickly?

1. **The number is even.**

2. **The number is not divisible by 4 or 6.**

3. **The sum of the digits is a prime number.**

4. **Subtract 1 from the number. The result is not prime.**

51	52	53	54	55	56	57	58	59
41	42	43	44	45	46	47	48	49
31	32	33	34	35	36	37	38	39
21	22	23	24	25	26	27	28	29
11	12	13	14	15	16	17	18	19

Answer on page 190.

Bank Robbery Alert (Part I)

A local bank was robbed! The bank has a poster up in its lobby, detailing what they know about the robbers. Read the page, then turn the page to answer questions.

Date: March 3, 2021

Time: 8:55 AM through 9:13 AM

Suspect descriptions:

All suspects were dressed in black, bulky clothes, and wore balaclavas

Suspect #1: 5'9", did not speak, carried a Beretta 92

Suspect #2: 5'10", spoke, presumed male based on voice, carried a Ruger GP100

Suspect #3: 5'11", did not speak, carried a Sig Sauer P365

Suspect #4: 5'8". Suspect 2 at one point said, "Terry (or Terri), get that bag," and Suspect #4 responded. Suspect #4 carried an unidentified handgun

Suspect #5: getaway driver, appeared female with long blonde hair

Getaway vehicle: Honda CRV, model year unknown, license plates unknown

Bank Robbery Alert (Part II)

(Do not read this until you have read the previous page!)

Date: _____

Time: _____

Suspect descriptions:

All suspects were: _____

Suspect #1: _____

_____

Suspect #2: _____

_____

Suspect #3: _____

_____

Suspect #4: _____

_____

Suspect #5: _____

Getaway vehicle: _____

Answers on page 191.

Wearing What?

Cryptograms are messages in substitution code. Break the code to read the message. For example, **THE SMART CAT** might become **FVO QWGDF JGF** if **F** is substituted for **T**, **V** for **H**, **O** for **E**, and so on.

AG 1969, FQKXZKZK FNKAZ XZNG

NKKAGMPHG ZOUNIZX YKHF IKAOHG

AG LZK INBNFNO. PLZ OZUHGX SHFNG

IQP HG PLZ FHOP SNGPZX EAOP, OLZ

SNO UNQMLP NGX XAZX AG IKAOHG.

Massive Manhunt

Track the escaped murderer across the country.

Answer on page 191.

Unscramble each word or phrase below to reveal a word or phrase related to disguises.

EACH MUST

HAYRIDE (2 words)

CAPABLE LABS (2 words)

HA RICE FAIL (2 words)

SAG LESS

AN AND BAN

LA LAVA CAB

DEBAR

UM PEAK

SUN BRIDES

RUM LABEL

PRO ALAS

G-Man Melvin Purvis

Every word in all capitals below is contained within the group of letters. Words can be found in a straight line horizontally, vertically, or diagonally. They may be read either forward or backward.

(Note: WORLD WAR is a single entry, with II not included in the search term.)

STANDING only 5'4" TALL, Melvin PURVIS was RENOWNED for CATCHING many famous CRIMINALS, including John DILLINGER, Baby FACE Nelson, and Pretty Boy FLOYD.

J. Edgar HOOVER was reportedly JEALOUS of the ATTENTION Purvis RECEIVED for the famous MANHUNTS. Local LAW enforcement also DISPUTED some of Purvis's CLAIMS, particularly in the ACCOUNT of what happened when Floyd was CAUGHT and killed.

MELVIN Purvis PUBLISHED a MEMOIR in 1936, after RESIGNING from the Federal Bureau of Investigation. He later SERVED as an INTELLIGENCE officer during WORLD WAR II.

```
N A D E H S I L B U P I H E P B
P A H F R I O M E M G K Q Y D T
S T A N D I N G C D Y O L F N J
D S W R E N O W N E D E H U A D
I L I A T J V N E I F H O P Y I
S A F V L J I Q G U H C E K H L
P N O P R V E S I H C C W L L L
U I M G L U E A L A O Q T M F I
T M J E N R P Y L S T O I A A N
E I M H V I H W E O M H V C C G
D R C E E A N K T G U I G E E E
L C D T A L L G N S D S A U R R
G L H L O D E V I E C E R L A H
A T T E N T I O N S K I H C C C
Q C S T N U H N A M E G F P Z U
B N X R A W D L R O W R O W T E
```

A Famous Attempt

Cryptograms are messages in substitution code. Break the code to read the message. For example, **THE SMART CAT** might become **FVO QWGDF JGF** if **F** is substituted for **T**, **V** for **H**, **O** for **E**, and so on.

LHFBY ACHHTI FBN DHCJSMHI OXFHMBOM

FBN ZCSB FBUXTB MIOFEMN FXOFJHFW

EHTICB TB 1962, QSMB JSMV QMHM FXX TB

JSMTH 30I. QSTXM JSMV FHM DMXTMPMN

JC SFPM NHCQBMN, JSM OFIM SFI BMPMH

DMMB CLLTOTFXXV OXCIMN.

Answer on page 191.

Track the Fugitive

The investigator is tracking the fugitive's past trips in order to find and recover information that was left behind in five cities. Each city was visited only once. Can you put together the travel timeline, using the information below?

1. **The fugitive went immediately from Australia's capital city to the site of its famous opera house.**

2. **Adelaide was visited after Melbourne, but not immediately after.**

3. **Perth was visited before Sydney, but with at least one stop in between.**

4. **Melbourne was not the second city visited.**

5. **Adelaide was not the final one.**

6. **Note: None of the cities named so far are Australia's capital city.**

Answer on page 191.

Motel Hideout

A thief hides out in one of the 45 motel rooms listed in the chart below. The motel's in-house detective received a sheet of four clues, signed "The Logical Thief." Using these clues, the detective found the room number within 15 minutes—but by that time, the thief had fled. Can you find the thief's motel room more quickly?

1. **The number is divisible by 3.**
2. **The number is not divisible by 6.**
3. **The first digit is equal to or larger than the second.**
4. **The sum of the digits is not 6.**

51	52	53	54	55	56	57	58	59
41	42	43	44	45	46	47	48	49
31	32	33	34	35	36	37	38	39
21	22	23	24	25	26	27	28	29
11	12	13	14	15	16	17	18	19

Answer on page 191.

Overheard Information (Part I)

Read the story below, then turn the page and answer the questions.

While on a train, a bystander overheard a conversation where one person was giving another the passwords for a set of underground gambling clubs. The bystander heard that the password for the downtown club was, "Do you have the blue cheese burger on the menu tonight?" At the near north location, the password was, "I've been looking forward to the cannoli all night; they never disappoint." At the east side location, the password is, "Are there sunflower seeds in the salad?" At the west side location, the password is, "Can I get the seafood lasagna with broccoli on the side instead of mixed vegetables?"

Overheard Information (Part II)

(Do not read this until you have read the previous page!)

As the undercover investigator charged with going into the clubs, you'll need to know the passwords the bystander relayed. How many do you remember?

West side: _____

Downtown: _____

Near north: _____

East side: _____

Answers on page 191.

First on the List

Cryptograms are messages in substitution code. Break the code to read the message. For example, **THE SMART CAT** might become **FVO QWGDF JGF** if **F** is substituted for **T**, **V** for **H**, **O** for **E**, and so on.

ZUHC MIZZVM OEIFUN EIDPVH NVMRVP

HVUMDX OTI PVGUPVN ZVEAHP ZUMN KIM

EAN VWJDIAON AH OEV 1920N UHP 1930N. IH

ZVAHS JUMIDVP, EV FQMPVMVP EAN TAKV

UHP OTI IK EVM ZMIOEVMN. EV ZVGUFV

OEV KAMNO JVMNIH JQO IH OEV KZA OVH

FINO TUHOVP DANO UHP TUN NJIOOVP ZX

UH UGLQUAHOUHGV TEI EUP NVVH EAN

JAGOQMV AH OEV DIGUD JUJVM.

Answer on page 192.

Order in the Court

The letters in ACQUITTAL can be found in boxes 1, 3, 4, 5, 14, 15, and 20, but not necessarily in that order. Similarly, the letters in all these words can be found in the boxes indicated. Your task is to insert all the letters of the alphabet into the boxes. If you do this correctly, the shaded cells will reveal another legal term.

Hint: Compare BAILIFF and PLAINTIFF to get the value of B, then BAILIFF to ACQUITTAL to get the value of F.

ACQUITTAL 1, 3, 4, 5, 14, 15, 20

BAILIFF 3, 4, 5, 17, 21

CASE 4, 6, 7, 20

COURTROOM 1, 2, 12, 14, 18, 20

DOCKET 1, 7, 16, 18, 20, 26

EXECUTION 1, 3, 7, 9, 11, 14, 18, 20

GAVEL 4, 5, 7, 22, 24

HUNG JURY 2, 10, 11, 13, 14, 22, 23

JUDGE 7, 10, 14, 16, 22

LAWYER 2, 4, 5, 7, 13, 25

OBJECTION 1, 3, 7, 10, 11, 17, 18, 20

OYEZ 7, 8, 13, 18

PLAINTIFF 1, 3, 4, 5, 11, 19, 21

VERDICTS 1, 2, 3, 6, 7, 16, 20, 24

1	2	3	4	5	6	7	8	9	10	11	12	13

14	15	16	17	18	19	20	21	22	23	24	25	26

Answer on page 192.

Track the Fugitive

The investigator is tracking the fugitive's past trips in order to find and recover information that was left behind in five cities. Each city was visited only once. Can you put together the travel timeline, using the information below?

1. Vancouver was not the final city visited.
2. Toledo was not the first city.
3. At least one other stop separated the visit to Seattle and the later visit to San Diego.
4. Either Seattle or Richmond was the second city visited.
5. Vancouver was visited before Seattle.
6. Richmond was visited immediately before Toledo.

Answer on page 192.

DNA Sequence

Examine the two images below carefully. Are these sequences a match or not?

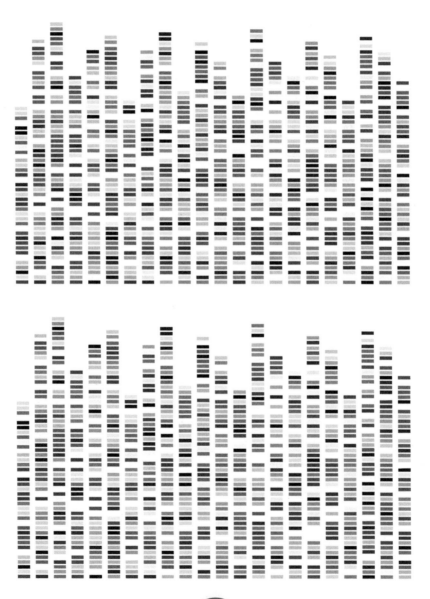

Answer on page 192.

Motel Hideout

A thief hides out in one of the 45 motel rooms listed in the chart below. The motel's in-house detective received a sheet of four clues, signed "The Logical Thief." Using these clues, the detective found the room number within 15 minutes—but by that time, the thief had fled. Can you find the thief's motel room more quickly?

1. **When you multiply the digits together, the resulting number is greater than 20.**

2. **The number is neither a multiple of 7 nor contains the digit 7.**

3. **The second digit is larger than the first by at least 3.**

4. **The sum of the digits is less than 12.**

51	52	53	54	55	56	57	58	59
41	42	43	44	45	46	47	48	49
31	32	33	34	35	36	37	38	39
21	22	23	24	25	26	27	28	29
11	12	13	14	15	16	17	18	19

Answer on page 192.

Robert Philip Hanssen

Every word in all capitals below is contained within the group of letters. Words can be found in a straight line horizontally, vertically, or diagonally. They may be read either forward or backward.

He was a **G-MAN** who **BETRAYED** his **COUNTRY** by **SPYING** on the **UNITED STATES** on behalf of the **SOVIET UNION** and later **RUSSIA**.

ROBERT Philip **HANSSEN** joined the Federal Bureau of Investigation in 1976. **THREE** short years **LATER**, he **OFFERED** his **SKILLS** to the Soviets and began commiting **ESPIONAGE** on and off **THROUGH** 2001. When **CAUGHT**, he said his **MOTIVES** were **FINANCIAL**.

MULTIPLE people **EXPRESSED** concern about some of Hanssen's **ACTIONS** while he was an active **SPY**, including his own **BROTHER-IN-LAW**, but they were always **IGNORED**.

Because of **VARIOUS** intelligence **LEAKS**, the FBI and CIA put together a team to **HUNT** down the **MOLE** or moles. Hanssen was put under **SURVEILLANCE** and "**PROMOTED**" to a **POSITION** where his "**ASSISTANT**" could **MONITOR** his actions. He was finally caught while doing a **DEAD DROP** and sent to **PRISON**.

O P S B S M A C D E A D D R O P E N
F L E R N L W F I N A N C I A L L F
W E T O T O L G R A I S S U R H O W
C A A T N M I I P C Y N T X Q J M U
M K T H A O L N K F O T O G M A N Y
U S S E T N X T U S F U H S D J F P
L D D R S I X M F T K T N G I K B S
T E E I I T F A D G E V H T U R I W
I R T N S O Q H N R N I H R R A P F
P E I L S R G I O S Y R V B E Y C X
L F N A A U Y B N I T H J O M E U B
E F U W O P E O R N H A N S S E N E
I O A R S R I E U D E R O N G I V T
J M H T T T H V S E V I T O M N R
R T J Y C A X C V A R I O U S E X A
E C N A L L I E V R U S Y A B F Z Y
D E T O M O R P E S P I O N A G E E
N O I T I S O P D E X P R E S S E D

When You Don't Want Your 15 Minutes of Fame

Cryptograms are messages in substitution code. Break the code to read the message. For example, **THE SMART CAT** might become **FVO QWGDF JGF** if **F** is substituted for **T**, **V** for **H**, **O** for **E**, and so on.

PDC ORZFCBP KQ PDC SCNW QENOP CLEOKYC

KQ PDC PCHCSEOEKJ ODKT "UICNEBU'O IKOP

TUJPCY" EJ 1988, YUSEY FUICO NKZCNPO DEY

EJ DEO ULUNPICJP QKN QKRN YUWO UQPCN

OCCEJA DEO BUOC LNKQEHCY KJ PCHCSEOEKJ.

UIKJA KPDCN BNEICO, NKZCNPO TUO

BKJSEBPCY KQ UNICY NKZZCNW UJY IRNYCN.

Answer on page 192.

Find the Fugitive

Track the fugitive from the entrance at the top of the maze to the exit at the bottom!

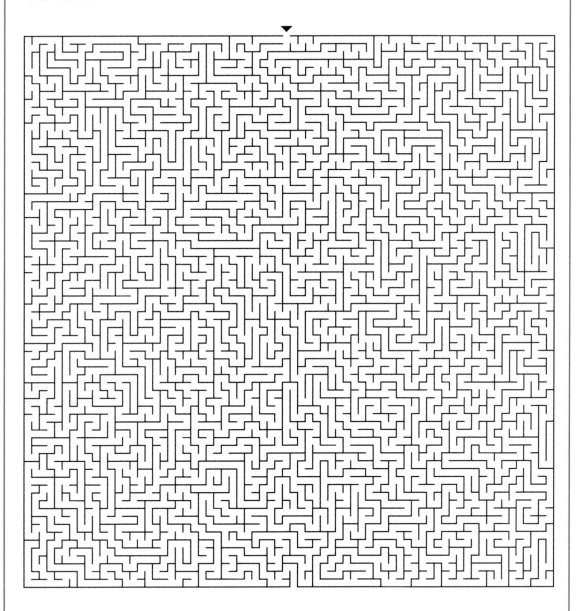

Answer on page 192.

Answer Key

Most Wanted (page 4)
Answers may vary. MOST, post, past, pant, WANT; also MOST, cost, cast, cant, WANT

Goes Free (page 4)
Answers may vary. GOES, foes, fees, feet, fret, FREE

Interception (page 5)
Take the first letter of each word to reveal: Charlotte, NC (North Carolina)

Escape the Building (page 6)

Crime Anagrams (page 7)
fugitive; captured; menace; post office; apprehended; field office; reward; prosecution

Call the Cops (pages 8-9)

Track the Fugitive (page 10)
The order is: Miami, San Francisco, Seattle, Chicago, Boston

DNA Sequence (page 11)

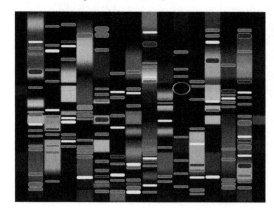

Answer Key

Most Wanted Word Search
(pages 12-13)

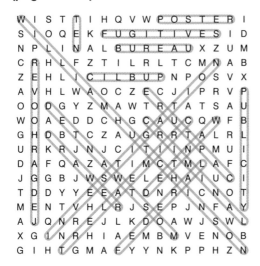

Find the Fugitive (page 20)

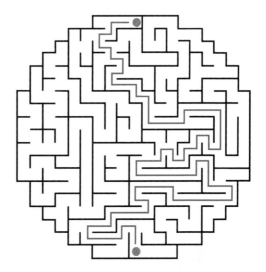

How It All Began (page 14)

William Kinsey Hutchinson was the editor-in-chief for the International News Service when he had a conversation with J. Edgar Hoover. The FBI Ten Most Wanted Fugitive List was born from that discussion. Years earlier, Hutchinson had also been a reporter at the famous Scopes trial.

Overheard Information (Part II)
(page 15-16)
1. B; 2. B; 3. A; 4. A

Seen at the Scene (Part II)
(page 17-18)
1. C; 2. B; 3. A

Motel Hideout (page 19)
The answer is 29.

Bank Robbery Alert (Part II)
(pages 21-22)
Date: October 15, 2020; Time: 9:45 AM; Suspect description: Male, 6'1", race unknown, hair and eye color unknown; Wore blue vinyl gloves and a mask with red wig and a red mustache and beard attached; Weapon: Ruger LCP II; Getaway vehicle: rust-colored mid-size four-door sedan, possibly a Toyota, model unknown; License plates: Michigan plates, partial number 346 (final three digits)

Track the Fugitive (page 23)
The order is: Seoul, Buenos Aires, Cairo, Paris, Prague

Discover the Alias (page 24)

1	2	3	4	5	6	7	8	9	10	11	12	13
J	X	K	Z	B	S	H	Q	W	F	P	G	U

14	15	16	17	18	19	20	21	22	23	24	25	26
Y	D	V	E	R	O	N	I	C	A	L	T	M

Answer Key

An Unwanted Record (page 25)

Victor Manuel Gerena spent 32 years on the Most Wanted list, longer than anyone else. Though he remains at large, he was removed from the list in 2016. He is wanted for armed robbery of a Wells Fargo depot.

Baddies of Fiction (pages 26-27)

L	A	V	A		F	E	N		E	M	I	T
E	V	I	L		L	E	E		P	E	P	A
D	I	E	T		Y	E	W		S	N	O	B
	S	W	E	E	N	E	Y	T	O	D	D	
		R	A	N		E	I	N				
M	I	N	E	R		R	A	J		K	E	G
F	R	E	D	D	Y	K	R	U	E	G	E	R
A	R	T		R	O	O		A	M	B	L	E
		H	U	G		O	N	O				
	N	O	R	M	A	N	B	A	T	E	S	
B	O	N	O		M	E	A		I	M	O	K
S	I	C	S		A	R	M		O	M	N	I
A	R	E	S		T	O	A		N	A	S	A

Track the Fugitive (page 28)

The order is: Indianapolis, Denver, New Orleans, Hartford, Portland

DNA Sequence (page 29)

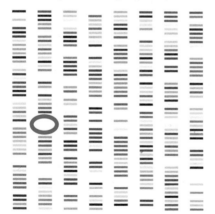

Hardly on the List At All (page 30)

Billie Austin Bryant spent hardly any time on the Most Wanted list, about two hours. Bryant, who had escaped from prison in 1968, robbed a bank in 1969, then shot and killed two FBI agents who were sent to capture him. He was placed on the Most Wanted list for those murders, but was apprehended that same day.

Track the Fugitive (page 31)

The order is: Jakarta, Perth, Johannesburg, Rio de Janeiro, New York

Richard Miller (pages 32-33)

Motel Hideout (page 34)

The answer is 16.

At the Top? (page 35)

Criminals are not ranked on the FBI Most Wanted List. Not only that, but there have sometimes been more than ten individuals on the list.

Answer Key

Park Pursuit (page 36)

The Fugitive Ran and Hid
(page 37)
Answers may vary. RAN, ban, bad, bid, HID, or RAN, man, mad, had, HID or RAN, ray, hay, had, HID or RAN, pan, pad, had, HID are all common options.

Find the Criminal (page 37)
Answers may vary. LOOK, hook, hood, food, fond, FIND.

Crime Anagrams (page 38)
kidnapping; armed robbery; car theft; sabotage; extortion; organized crime; drug trafficking; bombing

Overheard Information (Part II)
(pages 39–40)
1. A; 2. D; 3. D; 4. B

Track the Fugitive (page 41)
The order is: Atlanta, Milwaukee, Tampa, Pittsburgh, Chicago

Most Wanted Stats (page 42)
More than 500 people have been included on the list. While more than 90 percent of those listed have been caught, only about 160 were caught because of tips from the public.

DNA Sequence (page 43)

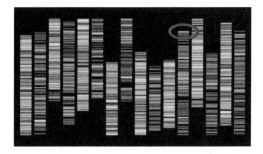

Motel Hideout (page 44)
The answer is 49.

Track the Fugitive (page 45)
The order is: San Jose, Boston, Charleston, Philadelphia, Omaha

Discover the Alias (page 46)

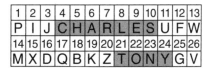

1	2	3	4	5	6	7	8	9	10	11	12	13
P	I	J	C	H	A	R	L	E	S	U	F	W

14	15	16	17	18	19	20	21	22	23	24	25	26
M	X	D	Q	B	K	Z	T	O	N	Y	G	V

Not a Ruthless Crime? (page 47)
Ruth Eisemann-Schier and her boyfriend kidnapped the daughter of a wealthy real estate developer for ransom in 1968. While her boyfriend was caught in short order, Ruth escaped capture for almost three months. She was the first woman placed on the Most Wanted list.

Answer Key

Track the Fugitive (page 48)
The order is: Copenhagen, Toronto, Mexico City, Ottawa, Oslo

The First of Seventeen (page 49)
The FBI credits the show "America's Most Wanted" with leading to the capture of seventeen fugitives. The very first episode resulted in viewer tips that brought about the capture of David James Roberts.

Find the Fugitive (page 50)

Interception (page 51)
Take the last letter of each word to reveal: Meet Monday Rogers Park

Donnie Brasco (pages 52-53)

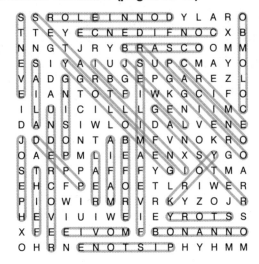

Track the Fugitive (page 54)
The order is: Paris, Vienna, Stockholm, Vaduz, Berlin

Seen at the Scene (Part II) (pages 55-56)
1. A; 2. C; 3. C

Motel Hideout (page 57)
The answer is 11.

Track the Fugitive (page 58)
The order is: Cape Town, Pretoria, Dakar, Gabarone, Nairobi

A Scary Partnership (page 59)
Thomas James Holden and Francis Keating were responsible for the Holden-Keating gang of armed robberies. Together, along with various accomplices, they robbed trains, banks, and a U.S. Mail truck.

Answer Key

The Fugitive Flees to France
(page 60)

1	2	3	4	5	6	7	8	9	10	11	12	13
M	A	R	I	E	B	T	Z	U	S	O	L	J

14	15	16	17	18	19	20	21	22	23	24	25	26
D	C	F	Y	V	Q	N	P	H	G	K	W	X

Overheard Information (Part II)
(pages 61-62)
1. A; 2. B; 3. C; 4; A

Couldn't You Be More Like Your Namesake? (page 63)
A young relative of Davy Crockett had the same name as his famous relation, but was an outlaw. He escaped justice in 1872, fleeing to a ranch.

DNA Sequence (page 64)

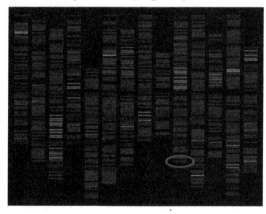

Not Quite a Wanted Poster
(page 65)
Famous for the corruption in his political machine, William "Boss" Tweed fled to Spain while on house arrest. He was caught because someone there recognized him due to political cartoons that skewered his corrupt "Tammany Hall" machine.

Motel Hideout (page 66)
The answer is 32.

Track the Fugitive (page 67)
The order is: Barcelona, Los Angeles, Seoul, Tokyo, New York

Heist Movies (pages 68-69)

Murder in Utah (page 70)
Francis Hermann was a pastor—and a murderer. Born circa 1850, he moved to the United States from England. His first two wives died under suspicious circumstances. Hermann later murdered two women in Salt Lake City. Not long after their deaths, he fled Salt Lake City and escaped justice, evading capture.

Motel Hideout (page 71)
The answer is 18.

Answer Key

Public Enemy #1: Alvin Karpis (pages 72-73)

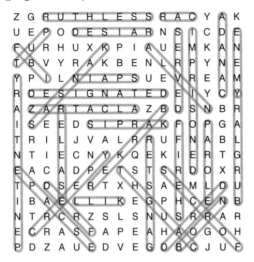

A Trusty Fellow (page 74)

William Nesbit, born in 1899 in Iowa, grew up to become a jewel thief (and a murderer, after he killed a fellow thief). Imprisoned, he became a chauffeur to the warden. He used his relative freedom to escape from prison in 1946. He was one of the first entrants on the FBI Most Wanted List, and was recaptured in 1950.

Catch the Suspect (page 75)

Fled the Area (page 76)

FLED, feed, seed, sped, aped, aged, ages, Ares, AREA

FBI Anagrams (page 77)

agent; J. Edgar Hoover; law enforcement; domestic; intelligence; jurisdiction; Quantico; analyst

Track the Fugitive (page 78)

The order is: Rome, Milan, Naples, Palermo, Florence

Bank Robbery Alert (Part II) (pages 79-80)

Date: January 8, 2021; Time: 2:17 to 2:33 PM; Suspect description: White male, 5'10", short brown hair, eye color unknown, wore a mask over the lower part of his face; White female, 5'5", shoulder-length layered brown hair, eye color unknown, wore sunglasses and a mask over the lower part of her face; A third suspect, description unknown, drove the getaway vehicle. Names: Male robber referred to woman as "Darling" and "Sweet Lily"; Weapons: Machine guns; Getaway vehicle: small-size SUV, black, license plates unknown

Where's the Fugitive? (page 81)

1	2	3	4	5	6	7	8	9	10	11	12	13
A	B	O	D	E	S	I	Y	U	R	T	F	C
14	15	16	17	18	19	20	21	22	23	24	25	26
N	P	H	M	W	K	L	V	G	Q	J	X	Z

A Short Time Free (page 82)

In his younger days, Ben Golden McCollum was a bank robber and escaped prisoner. Paroled in 1961 after a stint in prison, he died in 1963—the victim of burglars who entered his home.

Answer Key

Track the Fugitive (page 83)
The order is: Cardiff, Bath, York, Edinburgh, London

Interception (page 84)
In each word, find the letter that occurs twice, and you end up with: Three PM train to San Diego

Seen at the Scene (Part II)
(pages 85-86)
1. c; 2. True; 3. a

Overheard Information (Part II)
(pages 87-88)
1. B; 2. C; 3. A; 4. A

Motel Hideout (page 89)
The answer is 52.

Alaska Davidson (pages 90-91)

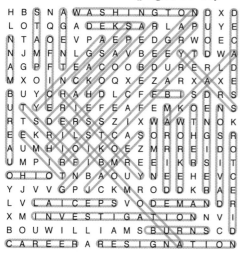

Murder in Colorado (page 92)
The Denver Strangler killed up to five women between 1894 and 1903. The killer may have murdered a clairvoyant who had supposedly given information to the authorities; she was found dead, strangled. Although several men were suspects, the Denver Strangler was never identified.

The Fugitive's Itinerary (page 93)

1	2	3	4	5	6	7	8	9	10	11	12	13
C	O	U	N	T	R	I	E	S	H	Y	Z	K
14	15	16	17	18	19	20	21	22	23	24	25	26
J	G	P	A	D	V	Q	B	L	M	W	F	X

Track the Fugitive (page 94)
The order is: Lima, Buenos Aires, Santiago, Quito, Rio de Janeiro

DNA Sequence (page 95)

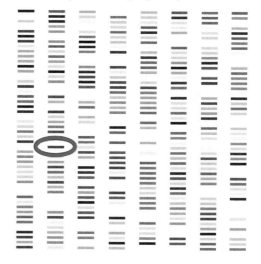

Motel Hideout (page 96)
The answer is 16.

Answer Key

Overheard Information (Part II) (pages 97-98)
1. A; 2. C; 3. B; 4. A

Good at Getting Free (page 99)
Murderer David Dallas Taylor escaped from prison no fewer than four times. He was added to the Most Wanted List in 1953 and was caught a few months later.

Catch the Suspect (page 100)

START

FINISH

Ways to Get Away (page 101)
run on foot; drive away; train ride; airplane; use a disguise; use an alias; get on a bus; blend in the crowd

Track the Fugitive (page 102)
The order is: Dallas, Denver, Portland, Austin, Nashville

Motel Hideout (page 103)
The answer is 36.

DNA Sequence (page 104)

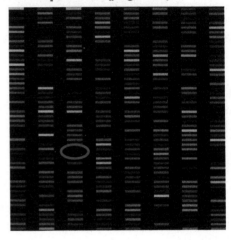

Making a List, Checking It Twice (page 105)
Nick George Montos ended up on the Most Wanted List not once but twice. Montos was a member of the Chicago Outfit. He was placed on the list following one robbery, and then added again after a prison escape.

Public Enemy #1: John Dillinger (pages 106-107)

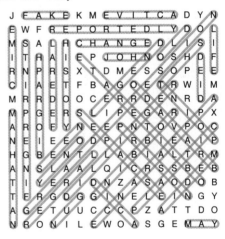

Answer Key

Find and Catch (page 108)
Answers may vary. FINDS, kinds, kings, sings, singe, since, wince, winch, witch, watch, CATCH (kinds and kings can easily be winds and wings)

Track the Fugitive (page 109)
The order is: Moscow, Tunis, Athens, Brussels, Ankara

Flee by Foot (page 110)

1	2	3	4	5	6	7	8	9	10	11	12	13
C	L	O	G	S	A	I	X	N	R	P	B	F

14	15	16	17	18	19	20	21	22	23	24	25	26
K	H	E	M	U	V	Z	W	T	D	Y	J	Q

Overheard Information (Part II) (pages 111-112)
1. A; 2. A; 3. A; 4. D

Murder in New Orleans (page 113)
In 1918 and 1919, a man with an axe terrorized New Orleans with his murders in the Italian-American community. His murder spree stopped abruptly, leaving the case unsolved forever.

Mystery Writers (pages 114-115)

D	R	U	P	E	■	N	A	O	M	I
R	I	G	I	D	■	U	S	H	E	R
J	O	H	N	G	R	I	S	H	A	M
■	■	■	T	E	A	S	■	I	S	A
D	E	W	S	■	C	A	N	■	■	■
O	V	A	■	C	O	N	C	A	V	E
H	A	R	L	A	N	C	O	B	E	N
A	N	N	E	T	T	E	■	L	T	D
■	■	T	A	E	■	S	E	S	S	■
E	P	A	■	L	U	L	L	■	■	■
K	A	T	H	Y	R	E	I	C	H	S
G	U	R	U	S	■	A	D	I	O	S
S	L	A	N	T	■	H	E	D	G	E

Interception (page 116)
Take the center letter of each place name and you will reveal that the criminal is hidden in Iowa.

Seen at the Scene (Part II) (pages 117-118)
1. B; 2. B; 3. False

Motel Hideout (page 119)
The answer is 27.

Mark Felt (pages 120-121)

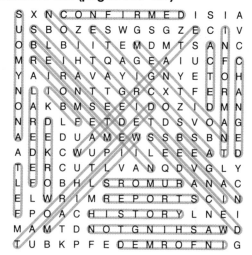

Track the Fugitive (page 122)
The order is: Seoul, Dodoma, Skopje, Riyadh, Stockholm

Answer Key

DNA Sequence (page 123)

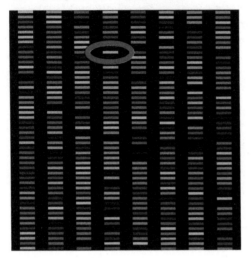

Murder at the Party (page 124)

1	2	3	4	5	6	7	8	9	10	11	12	13
C	O	R	S	A	G	E	Z	I	B	D	F	H

14	15	16	17	18	19	20	21	22	23	24	25	26
K	T	Y	W	P	Q	L	N	U	V	M	J	X

Overheard Information (Part II)
(pages 125-126)
1. Leo; 2. Golden Circle Plaza; 3. Tuesday, Thursday, and Saturday; 4. Didn't you used to have lemon bars for dessert?

Bank Robbery Alert (Part II)
(pages 127-128)
Date: November 18, 2020; Time: 4:56 PM; Suspect descriptions: Suspect #1: 5'8", short brown hair, wearing a mask of George Clooney. Tellers said that the voice seemed female. Suspect #2: 5'5", short blond hair (dyed with dark roots), wearing a mask of Brad Pitt. Tellers said that the voice could be male or female. Weapons: Machine guns. Getaway vehicle: motorcycles. Washington state license plates, partial plate N87

A Long Escape (page 129)
Frank Freshwaters was sentenced to prison after he accidentally killed a man while speeding. After serving some time, he was at an "honor farm" facility, which he then escaped in 1959. He was tracked down once in 1975 in West Virginia, but was released after his community and the state's governor vouched for him and disappeared again. He was found and arrested in 2015 but released 2016.

Find the Fugitive (page 130)

Motel Hideout (page 131)
The answer is 13.

Track the Fugitive (page 132)
The order is: Butte, Cleveland, Des Moines, San Diego, Sacramento

Murder in Georgia (page 133)
At least fifteen Atlanta women were murdered between 1909 and 1914 by a person dubbed the "Atlanta Ripper." The killer focused on young black women in their 20s. He was never caught.

Answer Key

Public Enemy #1: Baby Face Nelson (pages 134-135)

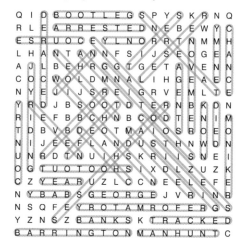

Describe the Criminal's Hairdo
(page 136)

1	2	3	4	5	6	7	8	9	10	11	12	13
P	L	A	I	T	S	K	E	R	U	Z	O	M

14	15	16	17	18	19	20	21	22	23	24	25	26
B	F	C	H	N	V	G	D	W	Y	J	Q	X

DNA Sequence (page 137)

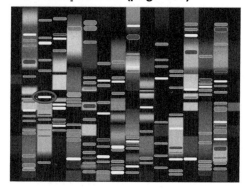

Fond of Robbing Banks (page 138)

A bank robber of the 1940s and 1950s, Frederick Grant Dunn was called "the Modern John Dillinger." After an escape from custody in 1958, he was added to the Most Wanted List. He was found dead from causes unknown in 1959.

Overheard Information (Part II)
(pages 139-140)

1. Zero $5 bills; 77 $10 bills; 42 $20 bills; 50 $50 bills, and 0 $100 bills; 2. 57-89-10; 3. Wednesday at 4 PM

Motel Hideout (page 141)

The answer is 17.

Track the Fugitive (page 142)

The order is: La Paz, Panama City, Caracas, Quito, Montevideo

A Successful Disappearance
(page 143)

Eleanor Jarman, born in Iowa, disappeared at the age of 39. In 1933, Jarman, her boyfriend, and another man tried to rob a clothing store. Jarman's accomplice shot the store owner. Jarman served seven years in prison before she escaped to see her family. From there she disappeared, communicating with her family via newspaper ads.

Answer Key

Robert B. Parker Books
(pages 144-145)

Escape or Not? (page 146)

Flees the Scene (page 147)
FLEES, flies, flips, slips, ships, shies, spies, spied, speed, spend, spent, scent, SCENE

Interception (page 148)
Take the first and last letter of each word and you will reveal: Inside orange vase

The Fugitive's Alias (page 149)

1	2	3	4	5	6	7	8	9	10	11	12	13
C	A	R	O	L	I	N	E	U	X	Z	S	T

14	15	16	17	18	19	20	21	22	23	24	25	26
Y	W	Q	J	K	G	B	D	V	M	P	H	F

Public Enemy #1: Pretty Boy Floyd (pages 150-151)

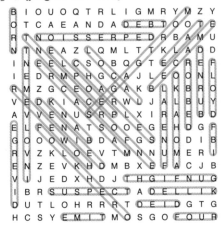

Track the Fugitive (page 152)
The order is: Riga, Oslo, Zagreb, Madrid, Warsaw

Seen at the Scene (Part II)
(pages 153-154)
1. B; 2. A; 3. False

DNA Sequence (page 155)

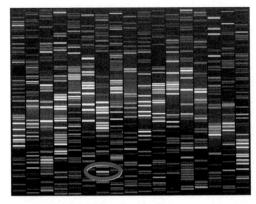

Motel Hideout (page 156)
The answer is 34.

Answer Key

Bank Robbery Alert (Part II)
(pages 157-158)
Date: March 3, 2021. Time: 8:55 AM through 9:13 AM. All suspects were dressed in black, bulky clothes, and wore balaclavas. Suspect #1: 5'9", did not speak, carried a Beretta 92. Suspect #2: 5'10", spoke, presumed male based on voice, carried a Ruger GP100. Suspect #3: 5'11", did not speak, carried a Sig Sauer P365. Suspect #4: 5'8". Suspect 2 at one point said, "Terry (or Terri), get that bag," and Suspect #4 responded. Suspect #4 carried an unidentified handgun. Suspect #5: getaway driver, appeared female with long blonde hair. Getaway vehicle: Honda CRV, model year unknown, license plates unknown

Wearing What? (page 159)
In 1969, murderer Marie Dean Arrington escaped from prison in her pajamas. The second woman put on the Most Wanted List, she was caught and died in prison.

Massive Manhunt (page 160)

Methods of Disguise (page 161)
mustache; hair dye; baseball cap; facial hair; glasses; bandanna; balaclava; beard; make-up; sideburns; umbrella; parasol

G-Man Melvin Purvis
(pages 162-163)

A Famous Attempt (page 164)
Frank Morris and brothers Clarence and John Anglin escaped Alcatraz prison in 1962, when they were all in their 30s. While they are believed to have drowned, the case has never been officially closed.

Track the Fugitive (page 165)
The order is: Melbourne, Perth, Adelaide, Canberra (Australia's capital city), Sydney

Motel Hideout (page 166)
The answer is 21.

Overheard Information (Part II)
(pages 167-168)
West side: "Can I get the seafood lasagna with broccoli on the side instead of mixed vegetables?" Downtown: "Do you have the blue cheese burger on the menu tonight?" Near north: "I've been looking forward to the cannoli all night; they never disappoint." East side: "Are there sunflower seeds in the salad?"

Answer Key

First on the List (page 169)

Bank robber Thomas Holden served nearly two decades behind bars for his exploits in the 1920s and 1930s. On being paroled, he murdered his wife and two of her brothers. He became the first person put on the FBI Ten Most Wanted List and was spotted by an acquaintance who had seen his picture in the local paper.

Order in the Court (page 170)

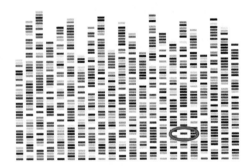

1	2	3	4	5	6	7	8	9	10	11	12	13
T	R	I	A	L	S	E	Z	X	J	N	M	Y
14	15	16	17	18	19	20	21	22	23	24	25	26
U	Q	D	B	O	P	C	F	G	H	V	W	K

Track the Fugitive (page 171)

The order is: Vancouver, Seattle, Richmond, Toledo, San Diego

DNA Sequence (page 172)

Motel Hideout (page 173)

The answer is 38.

Robert Philip Hanssen (pages 174-175)

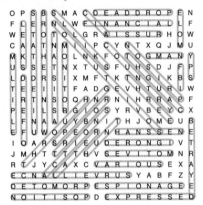

When You Don't Want Your 15 Minutes of Fame (page 176)

The subject of the very first episode of the television show "America's Most Wanted" in 1988, David James Roberts hid in his apartment for four days after seeing his case profiled on television. Among other crimes, Roberts was convicted of armed robbery and murder.

Find the Fugitive (page 177)

192